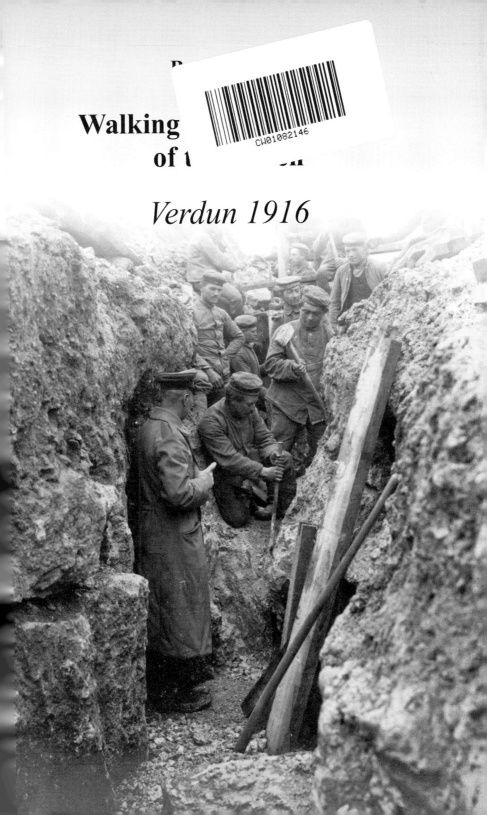

Walking
of t

Verdun 1916

Battleground Series

Stamford Bridge & Hastings *by* Peter Marren
Wars of the Roses - Wakefield/Towton by Philip A. Haigh
Wars of the Roses - Barnet by David Clark
Wars of the Roses - Tewkesbury by Steven Goodchild
Wars of the Roses - The Battles of St Albans by
Peter Burley, Michael Elliott & Harvey Wilson
English Civil War - Naseby by Martin Marix Evans, Peter Burton
and Michael Westaway
English Civil War - Marston Moor by David Clark
War of the Spanish Succession - Blenheim 1704 by James Falkner
War of the Spanish Succession - Ramillies 1706 by James Falkner
Napoleonic - Hougoumont by Julian Paget and Derek Saunders
Napoleonic - Waterloo by Andrew Uffindell and Michael Corum
Zulu War - Isandlwana by Ian Knight and Ian Castle
Zulu War - Rorkes Drift by Ian Knight and Ian Castle
Boer War - The Relief of Ladysmith by Lewis Childs
Boer War - The Siege of Ladysmith by Lewis Childs
Boer War - Kimberley by Lewis Childs

Mons *by* Jack Horsfall and Nigel Cave
Néry *by* Patrick Tackle
Retreat of I Corps 1914 *by* Jerry Murland
Aisne 1914 *by* Jerry Murland
Aisne 1918 *by* David Blanchard
Le Cateau *by* Nigel Cave and Jack Shelden
Walking the Salient *by* Paul Reed
Ypres - 1914 Messines *by* Nigel Cave and Jack Sheldon
Ypres - 1914 Menin Road *by* Nigel Cave and Jack Sheldon
Ypres - 1914 Langemarck *by* Jack Sheldonand Nigel Cave
Ypres - Sanctuary Wood and Hooge *by* Nigel Cave
Ypres - Hill 60 *by* Nigel Cave
Ypres - Messines Ridge *by* Peter Oldham
Ypres - Polygon Wood *by* Nigel Cave
Ypres - Passchendaele *by* Nigel Cave
Ypres - Airfields and Airmen *by* Mike O'Connor
Ypres - St Julien *by* Graham Keech
Ypres - Boesinghe *by* Stephen McGreal
Walking the Somme *by* Paul Reed
Somme - Gommecourt *by* Nigel Cave
Somme - Serre *by* Jack Horsfall & Nigel Cave
Somme - Beaumont Hamel *by* Nigel Cave
Somme - Thiepval *by* Michael Stedman
Somme - La Boisselle *by* Michael Stedman
Somme - Fricourt *by* Michael Stedman
Somme - Carnoy-Montauban *by* Graham Maddocks
Somme - Pozières *by* Graham Keech
Somme - Courcelette *by* Paul Reed
Somme - Boom Ravine *by* Trevor Pidgeon
Somme - Mametz Wood *by* Michael Renshaw
Somme - Delville Wood *by* Nigel Cave
Somme - Advance to Victory (North) 1918 *by* Michael Stedman
Somme - Flers *by* Trevor Pidgeon
Somme - Bazentin Ridge *by* Edward Hancock
Somme - Combles *by* Paul Reed
Somme - Beaucourt *by* Michael Renshaw
Somme - Redan Ridge *by* Michael Renshaw
Somme - Hamel *by* Peter Pedersen
Somme - Villers-Bretonneux *by* Peter Pedersen
Somme - Airfields and Airmen *by* Mike O'Connor
Airfields and Airmen of the Channel Coast *by* Mike O'Connor
In the Footsteps of the Red Baron *by* Mike O'Connor
Arras - Airfields and Airmen *by* Mike O'Connor
Arras - The Battle for Vimy Ridge *by* Jack Sheldon & Nigel Cave
Arras - Vimy Ridge *by* Nigel Cave
Arras - Gavrelle *by* Trevor Tasker and Kyle Tallett
Arras - Oppy Wood *by* David Bilton
Arras - Bullecourt *by* Graham Keech
Arras - Monchy le Preux *by* Colin Fox
Walking Arras *by* Paul Reed
Hindenburg Line *by* Peter Oldham
Hindenburg Line - Epehy *by* Bill Mitchinson
Hindenburg Line - Riqueval *by* Bill Mitchinson
Hindenburg Line - Villers-Plouich *by* Bill Mitchinson
Hindenburg Line - Cambrai Right Hook *by* Jack Horsfall & Nigel Cave
Hindenburg Line - Cambrai Flesquières *by* Jack Horsfall & Nigel Cave
Hindenburg Line - Saint Quentin *by* Helen McPhail and Philip Guest
Hindenburg Line - Bourlon Wood *by* Jack Horsfall & Nigel Cave

Cambrai - Airfields and Airmen *by* Mike O'Connor
Aubers Ridge *by* Edward Hancock
La Bassée - Neuve Chapelle *by* Geoffrey Bridger
Loos - Hohenzollern Redoubt *by* Andrew Rawson
Loos - Hill 70 *by* Andrew Rawson
Fromelles *by* Peter Pedersen
The Battle of the Lys 1918 *by* Phil Tomaselli
Accrington Pals Trail *by* William Turner
Poets at War: Wilfred Owen *by* Helen McPhail and Philip Guest
Poets at War: Edmund Blunden *by* Helen McPhail and Philip Guest
Poets at War: Graves & Sassoon *by* Helen McPhail and Philip Guest
Gallipoli *by* Nigel Steel
Gallipoli - Gully Ravine *by* Stephen Chambers
Gallipoli - Anzac Landing *by* Stephen Chambers
Gallipoli - Suvla August Offensive *by* Stephen Chambers
Gallipoli - Landings at Helles *by* Huw & Jill Rodge
Walking the Gallipoli *by* Stephen Chambers
Walking the Italian Front *by* Francis Mackay
Italy - Asiago *by* Francis Mackay
Verdun: Fort Douaumont *by* Christina Holstein
Verdun: Fort Vaux *by* Christina Holstein
Walking Verdun *by* Christina Holstein
Verdun: The Left Bank *by* Christina Holstein
Zeebrugge & Ostend Raids 1918 *by* Stephen McGreal

Germans at Beaumont Hamel *by* Jack Sheldon
Germans at Thiepval *by* Jack Sheldon

SECOND WORLD WAR

Dunkirk *by* Patrick Wilson
Calais *by* Jon Cooksey
Boulogne *by* Jon Cooksey
Saint-Nazaire *by* James Dorrian
Walking D-Day *by* Paul Reed
Atlantic Wall - Pas de Calais *by* Paul Williams
Atlantic Wall - Normandy *by* Paul Williams
Normandy - Pegasus Bridge *by* Carl Shilleto
Normandy - Merville Battery *by* Carl Shilleto
Normandy - Utah Beach *by* Carl Shilleto
Normandy - Omaha Beach *by* Tim Kilvert-Jones
Normandy - Gold Beach *by* Christopher Dunphie & Garry Johnson
Normandy - Gold Beach Jig *by* Tim Saunders
Normandy - Juno Beach *by* Tim Saunders
Normandy - Sword Beach *by* Tim Kilvert-Jones
Normandy - Operation Bluecoat *by* Ian Daglish
Normandy - Operation Goodwood *by* Ian Daglish
Normandy - Epsom *by* Tim Saunders
Normandy - Hill 112 *by* Tim Saunders
Normandy - Mont Pinçon *by* Eric Hunt
Normandy - Cherbourg *by* Andrew Rawson
Normandy - Commandos & Rangers on D-Day *by* Tim Saunders
Das Reich – Drive to Normandy *by* Philip Vickers
Oradour *by* Philip Beck
Market Garden - Nijmegen *by* Tim Saunders
Market Garden - Hell's Highway *by* Tim Saunders
Market Garden - Arnhem, Oosterbeek *by* Frank Steer
Market Garden - Arnhem, The Bridge *by* Frank Steer
Market Garden - The Island *by* Tim Saunders
Rhine Crossing – US 9th Army & 17th US Airborne *by* Andrew Rawson
British Rhine Crossing – Operation Varsity *by* Tim Saunders
British Rhine Crossing – Operation Plunder *by* Tim Saunders
Battle of the Bulge – St Vith *by* Michael Tolhurst
Battle of the Bulge – Bastogne *by* Michael Tolhurst
Channel Islands *by* George Forty
Walcheren *by* Andrew Rawson
Remagen Bridge *by* Andrew Rawson
Cassino *by* Ian Blackwell
Anzio *by* Ian Blackwell
Dieppe *by* Tim Saunders
Fort Eben Emael *by* Tim Saunders
Crete – The Airborne Invasion *by* Tim Saunders
Malta *by* Paul Williams
Bruneval Raid *by* Paul Oldfield
Cockleshell Raid *by* Paul Oldfield

Battleground

Walking in the Footsteps of the Fallen

Verdun 1916

Christina Holstein

Series Editor
Nigel Cave

Pen & Sword
MILITARY

For Frédéric Radet and all those who labour, unrecognised,
to keep the memory alive in such a special way.

First published in Great Britain in 2019 by
Pen & Sword Military
an imprint of
Pen & Sword Books Ltd, 47 Church Street
Barnsley, South Yorkshire, S70 2AS

ISBN 978 152671 704 7

A CIP catalogue record for this book is
available from the British Library.

Typeset in Times New Roman by Chic Graphics

Printed and bound in England by
TJ International Ltd, Padstow, Cornwall

Pen & Sword Books Ltd incorporates the imprints of
Pen & Sword Archaeology, Atlas, Aviation, Battleground, Discovery,
Family History, History, Maritime, Military, Naval, Politics,
Railways, Select, Social History, Transport, True Crime,
Claymore Press, Frontline Books, Leo Cooper, Praetorian Press,
Remember When, Seaforth Publishing and Wharncliffe.

For a complete list of Pen & Sword titles please contact
PEN & SWORD BOOKS LIMITED
47 Church Street, Barnsley, South Yorkshire, S70 2AS, England
E-mail: enquiries@pen-and-sword.co.uk
Website: www.pen-and-sword.co.uk

Contents

Acknowledgements

In preparing this work I have once again been helped by the generosity of friends whose knowledge of the events of 1916 are second to none. I am grateful to Jan Carel Broek-Roelofs, Wim Degrande, Tom Gudmestad, Pierre Lenhard, Marcus Massing and Harry van Baal for providing information and allowing me to use photographs from their collections. I would not have found the memorial to Privates Salamite and Ruèche without Frederic Radet, whose determination to prevent the men of Verdun from being forgotten leads him almost single-handedly to clear undergrowth and paths. Special thanks go to Marie-Odile and Philippe Delaunay, http://delaunay-kourou.over-blog.com, who kindly sent photos from Cayenne and helped me with the translation of the Creole inscription on Saint-Just Borical's grave. The map tiles for tour maps 1 and 3 came from Openstreetmap.org. As always, responsibility for errors is mine alone.

Author's Note

Visitors to Verdun on hot summer days may have difficulty in imagining that a battle was ever fought there. The Memorial has an interesting collection of artefacts and photos, the major forts can be visited, visitors can linger in the military cemetery and admire – or not – the Ossuary, but the central area of mown grass, neat roads, and tourist buses is not where the battle lives. That is in the forests, where trenches and dugouts, bunkers and camps, gun pits and concrete, still tell the story of the unimaginable – and to a modern visitor almost unbelievable – events of 100 years ago.

The Ossuary, the French memorial to the men who fought the Battle of Verdun. The chambers below the building house scattered bones, both French and German. *Author's collection*

German bunker in Bois des Caures, one of a series of named defences constructed in 1918. This one is *Hai* (shark). *Author's collection*

The aim of the walking tours in this book is to take the visitor away from the main sites and along marked tracks into the forest to see what memories remain of the men who fought the Battle of Verdun. Most of the memorials you will see are French. After the war the German battlefield cemeteries were cleared and the grave markers, often beautifully carved, were removed. But here and there in the forest a stone remains, sometimes broken, often overgrown and difficult to read, but still bearing witness to a life lost in 1916. Tours 1 and 2 cover sectors defended by units of XXX Corps as they fought to resist the German assault in the first days of the battle. Tours 3 and 4 cover the period March – October 1916 when the battle had become a slogging match in which, for the men on both sides, mere survival was surely what mattered most.

A broken German gravestone commemorating Otto Schneidereit, 8 Company, Infantry Regiment 24, formerly in Herbebois but now missing. *Harry van Baal*

A rare remnant of a former German cemetery. Willi Tietz, 10 (Flamethrower) Company, 3. Garde-Pionier-Bataillon, died on 23 February 1916 and was buried in Bois Ormont. *Jan Carel Broek Roelofs*

Series Editor's Introduction

Over recent years there has been a determined effort by the authorities to make key sites at Verdun more accessible. In many ways this should be applauded, for anything that makes the scale of the heroic sacrifice – willing or not – of the soldiers of Verdun is surely to be welcomed.

This book is an important companion to the visitor who seeks to go beyond what often appear to be these unconnected places at Verdun. The series of meticulously planned walks connects features and positions that were of considerable importance in the Battle, making sense of a battlefield which, thanks to the decision to forest great stretches of it, is very difficult to understand on the ground today. During the walks there are explanations of the reasons for and the significance of the numerous reminders of the war that will be encountered, such as trenches and remaining concrete works and fortifications.

Christina has made use of the eloquent but often sadly neglected field graves and memorials that are to be found on the routes to the soldiers of both sides, effectively markers of the long months of the battle, fought in the most dire of conditions. These memorials, all but forgotten over the decades, bring us closer to the individuals (and their units) who were thrown into the fight and the action which resulted in their death: too often their story gets lost by the sheer weight of the overwhelming, cruel, monstrous casualty statistics.

As Jean Norton Cru pointed out in his magnificent book on French memoirs that were published during the war or in the early post war years, the 'true Verdun' lies beyond, 'where the battle remains congealed amidst the ruins'. Therefore, I recommend that you start by reading and pondering what Cru has to say (pp. 153–154); it is deeply moving and should immediately provide an important reason why *Walking in the Footsteps of the Fallen* has such value for the committed battlefield tourer.

People who move beyond the 'classic tour' do so for a range of reasons: seeking a better understanding of the Battle, its various stages and the topography that often explains why both sides fought so fiercely to secure a particular location; maybe they have an interest in following a particular unit or formation, tracing an ancestor, or developing their interest in the Battles of Verdun or of the Western Front in general – the motives are legion.

After fifty years of coming out to the Western Front, and over and above a desire to understand the Battle and its evolution, a growing appeal for me has been walking over the ground where so much tragedy and bravery, so much heroism against seemingly impossible odds, so much extraordinary endeavour to provide defences, logistic support and deployment of men and guns, took place over a century ago.

The regular battlefield visitor, I suspect, gets an almost spiritual connection with the men of 1914-1918. Such a visitor will usually be travelling alone or in a small group and will be coming for at least a few days rather than as part of a single day coach party tour that, inevitably, follows Cru's 'classic tour' of the Verdun battlefield or the equivalent elsewhere on the Front. The big scale actions become increasingly less significant and the desire to get to the silent, brooding parts of a battlefield becomes ever stronger, allowing a closer connection to the soldiers of 1916.

The vestiges of the fighting, the cemeteries and the field graves that are found away from the thousands that crowd Fleury and Douamont, illustrate the battle and its nature. Here there is tranquillity and atmosphere, a feeling of isolation and yet of being in the presence of thousands. We cannot begin to compare ourselves with Jean Norton Cru, who served almost the whole length of the war, a high proportion of it in the trenches, divorced as we are from almost the entire gamut of the realities for the soldier of those times. Yet the result of time in these rarely visited, neglected, in many ways all but abandoned locations is what provides the essential background to a more coherent understanding of the men of 1914-18.

Development of key parts of the battlefields will inevitably bring infrastructure and the sort of requirements that are demanded (and even required) these days. Modern museums and exhibitions will often plug a message, overtly or more subtly, that is appropriate to the contemporary, received view. Going off such a circuit leaves the visitor to ponder alone; yet although there may be plenty of stark reminders of the conflict, there are no handy explanations to inform. What this book does is to take you by means of carefully constructed tours and so place that isolated grave, that bunker almost lost in the undergrowth, that clearly discernible trench line into the narrative of the battle and the story of the individuals immediately involved. The more and the better the information one has the greater the appreciation becomes of the issues at stake in particular locations and of those who fought, suffered and, alas, all too often died there.

This book will speak powerfully to anyone who wishes to deepen their understanding of a Battle that has had such a profound impact on the generations that followed.

Nigel Cave
Ratcliffe College, 2019

Setting the Scene

On Easter Sunday 2011 an unsigned letter delivered to the Ossuary, the mighty French memorial to the Battle of Verdun, described where in the deep woods in front of the destroyed village of Fleury-devant-Douaumont human bones had been seen. A careful excavation revealed, in addition to extensive remains, an identity disc bearing the name Borical and a service number, 2790. Saint-Just Louis Borical, 119th Infantry Regiment, a native of Cayenne, had been found almost ninety-five years after he disappeared on 3 June 1916.

The grave of Private Saint-Just Borical in Cayenne. *Marie-Odile and Philippe Delaunay*

Private Borical was only one of the 176 men of the 119th Infantry who went missing in action on that day. He was 28 years old. On 1 June, his regiment, which had been in reserve, was moved up to support the 5th and 24th Infantry Regiments, which had recently suffered devastating losses. At 2am on 3 June 1916 Borical and his comrades attempted to retake the positions on the light railway embankment lost two days earlier. The operation was a failure. Advancing in three waves, they ran into such an overwhelming barrage of fire that progress was impossible, and with dead and wounded men all around them the survivors returned to their starting point. No further progress was made and when the 119th was finally withdrawn on 7 June the regiment had lost 734 men. Two hundred and forty eight of them had simply disappeared.

The battle in which Private Borical disappeared was fought on both sides of the River Meuse over terrain comprising hills and deep valleys. On the western side of the river (the Left Bank), the ground is open and rolling and the hills rarely exceed 300 metres in height. On the eastern side (the Right Bank) the country is more rugged. Here, a limestone plateau divided by deep valleys and dotted in 1916 with areas of dense woodland rises to 388 metres before dropping sharply to a marshy plain. Between the two lies the meandering and flood prone valley of the River Meuse. It was perfect defensive terrain and following the defeat of France in the Franco-Prussian War of 1870-1871 and the German annexation of the eastern provinces of Alsace and Lorraine it was heavily fortified, as France embarked on a complete overhaul of her frontier defences. Verdun, which was a *place forte* (fortress) under the command of an independent military governor, was part of the overhaul; by 1914 the city was surrounded by two rings of mutually supporting forts and fieldworks and a huge network of supporting elements. With over 1000 guns of various calibres in position when war was declared,

Crown Prince William of Germany. *Author's collection*

plus almost 300 machine guns, and a garrison of over 60,000 men, Verdun was too tough a nut to crack and in the first weeks of the war the German Fifth Army, commanded by Crown Prince William of Germany, tried to pinch it out. When the attempt failed the Germans retired to lines forming a wide salient and out of range of the guns. Verdun became a quiet sector, and the French High Command soon began to transfer the resources of the fortress to more active parts of the front. This process accelerated in August 1915 when the French Commander-in-Chief, General Joffre, downgraded the status of Verdun from a fortress to a mere fortified region and brought the resources under his own command.

General Joffre, French Commander-in-Chief in 1916. *Author's collection*

The French defences on the Right Bank followed the high ground. In closest contact with the enemy, at distances varying from 1500 metres to a mere twenty-five metres, was the first position. This ran for twelve kilometres between two villages, Brabant-sur-Meuse on the French left and Ornes on the right, following the hilltops and making use of four extensive forests: Bois de Haumont, Bois des Caures, Bois de Ville and Herbebois. It comprised a series of centres of resistance, each with its own garrison and command post, and included trenches, dugouts and machine gun emplacements backed, in certain areas, by concrete redoubts. Wide gaps between the centres of resistance provided clear sight lines and fields of fire, and each one was linked to the next by wire and secondary defences. Behind it, two more defensive positions protected the main line of resistance, which included the two most important forts in the Verdun system, Fort Douaumont and Fort Vaux. But while all this was impressive on paper, in reality the withdrawal of men and resources meant that existing defences had fallen into disrepair and planned defences were unfinished. Protests brought a parliamentary commission and some improvements were made, but limited manpower and heavy rain prevented much from being done. By then German intentions were clear: aerial observers reported naval guns arriving at stations in the rear, camps being constructed, dugouts excavated, new gun batteries and ammunition dumps created, important troop concentrations, and many more German planes in the air. There were also deserters, mostly Silesian Poles who were tired of the war, or men from annexed Lorraine – native Frenchmen under German rule who had no wish to fight against their former countrymen.

Fort Douaumont in February 1916. *Author's collection*

When the Germans attacked the Right Bank on 21 February 1916 the French resources available to meet the shock were the 72nd and 51st Infantry Division, XXX Corps, commanded by General Chrétien, with two more divisions in general reserve to the south of Verdun. They were supported by 131 field guns, mostly quick firing 75s, and 140 heavy guns of an old model and slow firing. A small number of long-range naval guns also stood ready. Facing them were three German army corps – VII Reserve Corps on the German right, XVIII Corps in the centre and III Corps on the left – with six divisions in the front line supported by pioneers and flamethrowers, two divisions in the second line, and two additional divisions in reserve. In the weeks before the offensive was launched over twelve hundred modern rapid-fire guns and howitzers, many of them

General Chrétien.
Author's collection

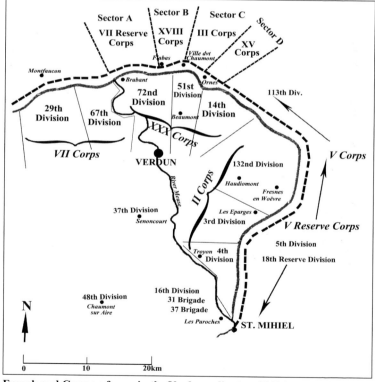

French and German forces in the Verdun salient on 21 February 1916.

heavy or super heavy, had been brought to Verdun from all parts of the front and established in carefully prepared and camouflaged positions alongside huge ammunition dumps. Over 150 trench mortars completed the array. All this was along a twelve kilometre front; nothing like it had been seen before on the Western Front.

The aim of the German offensive was to force France out of the war by attacking her at a place she would not abandon and which she would defend to the last of her reserves. For General Erich von Falkenhayn, the Chief of the German General Staff, Verdun, formerly the most important fortress in eastern France, standing astride the road from annexed Lorraine into the heart of France, was such a place. As originally planned, the Verdun offensive was to be a limited one using overwhelming firepower but relatively small numbers of men. A preliminary bombardment of unheard of strength was to be followed by a crushing infantry assault along a narrow front in the centre of the Right Bank. The weight of shells would destroy all opposition, allowing the attacking infantry to advance quickly to certain strategic heights overlooking the city, where they would stop. The guns would move forward to destroy the expected counter attacks and France, with casualty levels rocketing, her reserves annihilated, and no prospect of victory, would seek terms. With France out of the picture, Germany could then gather all her forces to defeat Britain and bring the war to an end. Success was to be achieved quickly; the offensive was scheduled to begin on 12 February 1916 and a victory parade

General Erich von Falkenhayn, Chief of the German General Staff. *Author's collection*

Kaiser Wilhelm II, the head of the German armed forces. *Author's collection*

in Verdun had been planned for Kaiser Wilhelm II, the head of the German armed forces, on 28 February, just sixteen days later. This was not to be a long drawn out slogging match but a quick success.

Naturally, things did not go according to plan. The strategic heights which General von Falkenhayn intended the assault troops to reach in February 1916 were held by the Froideterre fieldwork, Fort Souville and Fort Tavannes. It took from 21 February to 23 June for the Germans to reach Froideterre and they did not hold it. They reached the glacis of Fort

The barracks at the Ouvrage de Froideterre. *Author's collection*

Souville on 12 July and were driven back; they did not reach Fort Tavannes. By the time they set foot on Fort Souville General von Falkenhayn, stretched to the utmost to meet threats in Russia, Italy and on the Somme, had ordered the Fifth Army to go on the defensive; but the French went on attacking and far from being a quick campaign it was 300 days before the fighting ceased. The battle resulted in over 700,000 French and German casualties and the French continued the war.

An aerial view of Fort Tavannes. *Author's collection*

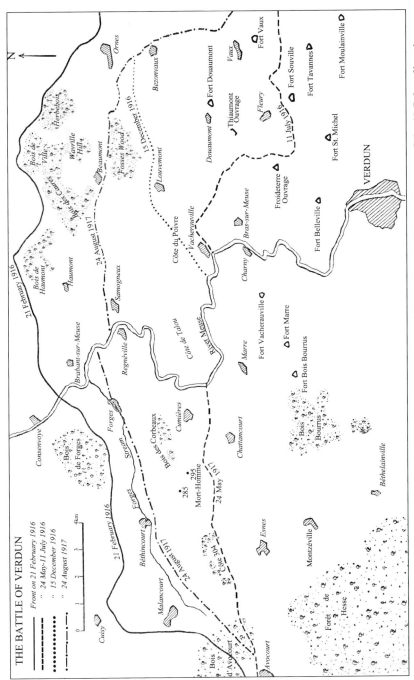

The Battle of Verdun. The distance from the start line of 21 February 1916 in Bois de Ville to the apex of the 11 July salient is a little over 10 kilometres as the crow flies.

THE BATTLE OF VERDUN

Front on 21 February 1916
" 24 May–11 July 1916
" 15 December 1916
" 24 August 1917

N

0 1 2 3 4km

Bois d'Avocourt
Cuisy
Malancourt
Avocourt
Béthincourt
21 February 1916
Côte 304
24 August 1917
Esnes
285 295
Mort-Homme
24 May 1917
Montzéville
Forêt de Hesse
Béthelainville
Bois de Forges
Forges
Bois des Corbeaux
Cumières
Chattancourt
Bois Bourrus
Fort Bois Bourrus
Consenvoye
Forges Stream
Regnéville
Brabant-sur-Meuse
21 February 1916
Bois de Haumont
Haumont
Samogneux
Côte de Talou
River Meuse
Marre
Fort Vacherauville
Fort Marre
Bois de Ville
Herbebois
Wavrille Hill
Bois des Caures
Fosses Wood
Beaumont
24 August 1917
Côte du Poivre
Vacherauville
15 December 1916
Louvemont
Charny
Bras-sur-Meuse
Froideterre Ouvrage
Fort Belleville
VERDUN
Ornes
Bezonvaux
Fort Douaumont
Douaumont
Thiaumont Ouvrage
Fleury
11 July 1916
Fort St. Michel
Vaux
Fort Vaux
Fort Souville
Fort Tavannes
Fort Moulainville

The splendid granite memorial to Louis Auguste Baudoin, telephonist with the 4th Zouaves, who died with his comrades on 5 August 1916. *Author's collection*

The very simple memorial to Private Albert Fraikin, 412th Infantry, who was killed on 20 August 1917 in the major French offensive of that year. *Author's collection*

No one knows exactly how many men who went missing in action during the Battle of Verdun, although the most reliable figures put the combined number of men killed and wounded at 713,000. The French estimate their missing at 101,000 but there is no specific German figure for the men who disappeared. After the war the field burials and provisional cemeteries scattered all over the battlefield were gradually cleared, but many men were never found and although a few families could afford to erect a memorial to their lost son, most could not. Over the years many of these private memorials have been lost or broken, but thanks to recent efforts to find and restore them by a small number of dedicated local historians it is again possible to remember the men and the actions in which they gave their lives. Recently, some French and German families have also planted simple unofficial memorials in places where they believe their forebears to have died. Little by little, the forgotten men of Verdun are being remembered.

Building and forestry work continue to bring up human remains but it is rare for them to be easily identifiable. Of the twenty six French

A family memorial planted recently in the ditch of Fort Souville and commemorating Private Fernand Leprestre, 5 Company, 28th Infantry, who died resisting the German offensive of 1 June which broke the French line in Ravin de Bazil. *Author's collection*

soldiers found at Fleury-devant-Douaumont in 2013 only seven could be identified. Two were returned to their places of origin while the others were laid to rest in the military cemetery in front of the Ossuary. A German soldier found in March 2014 close to the destroyed village of Haumont was not only identified by name – Hans Winckelmann – but, thanks to strenuous efforts by a local historian, buried close to his brother, Karl, in the German cemetery at Romagne-sous-Montfaucon. Recently, specialists from the Gendarmerie de Paris used the skull of a French soldier found with two other men in 2013 to produce an identikit image of his face so that his descendants could identify their ancestor on a group photo. On a brilliantly sunny day in February 2018, Sergeant Claude Fournier, 134th Infantry, who died at Fleury on 4 August 1916, was buried with his companions in misfortune in front of the Ossuary. He lies in plot 518.

Not everyone is so fortunate. Despite investigation, no family could be found for Saint-Just Louis Borical. In October 2011 he was awarded a posthumous Croix de Guerre and at the request of the local authorities returned to Cayenne for burial, one man out of the many thousands who knew the hell of battle and who, finally, came home.

Musketier Hans Winckelmann, whose body was found in March 2014, was buried in the German cemetery of Romagne-sous-Montfaucon a short distance from his brother, Karl. *Author's collection*

Introduction to the Tours

GPS waypoints
These have been included because the tours visit isolated areas and the deep forest cover makes orientation difficult. The waypoints appear as bracketed numbers in the text and as bolded numbers on the maps. The full GPS references are gathered in a section at the end of each tour, because to include them within the text would break up the flow.

Maps
1. For the general area: IGN (Orange Series) Meuse 55.

2. For a close study of the areas covered by these tours the most useful maps are those published by the French *Institut Géographique National* (IGN).
   For preference, choose the special battlefield map **IGN 3112 ET** *Forêts de Verdun et du Mort-Homme; Champ de Bataille de Verdun*. This 1/25.000 map is produced by the *Office National des Forêts*.

   If you cannot find a copy of this map **IGN 1/25.000 Blue Series 3212 *Ouest*** will allow you to follow the tours without difficulty.

These maps are normally available at the main battlefield sites. IGN maps are available from their website on http://www.ign.fr and from various internet outlets. **Note:** the current version of IGN 3112ET does not show the forest block numbers used in the walks described in this book but older versions of the map, which do show them, may be found on the internet.

The newly extended *Mémorial de Verdun*, a museum and resource centre at the heart of the battlefield. *Author's collection*

Warning: At all times visitors should remain on the paths and stay away from the edges of holes. In an ideal world, the tours would be made by two or more people, as by their nature most of them are in areas where not many people go; should some incident happen – a fall or whatever – a companion provides added security. **Do not walk where heavy logging equipment is in use.**

Collecting 'souvenirs', digging or using metal detectors are absolutely prohibited and subject to heavy fines. Forts, shelters, dugouts and other positions are dangerous and should not be entered. Live ammunition, shells, grenades and mortar bombs should not be touched under any circumstances.

Shells brought up by autumn ploughing in 2017. *Author's collection*

Tour No. 1

21–24 February 1916
Bois des Caures, Beaumont and Wavrille Hill

Distance: Approximately 7 kilometres
Duration: A half day's tour, allowing plenty of time for photographs
Maps: IGN 3112ET or IGN Blue Series 3112 Ouest.

Circular tour beginning in Bois des Caures at command post R2, continuing to Beaumont and returning via Wavrille Hill.

Memorials on this tour: Lieutenant Colonel Emile Driant, Major Etienne Renouard, 1st Gunner/Driver Julien Quenet, Sergeant Charles Flipo, Private Henri Michelet and Erwin Müller.

There is an uphill stretch of 500 metres to the top of Wavrille Hill but the rest of the tour is mostly level or downhill. Parts of the tour are likely to be **extremely muddy and wet** throughout the year, particularly the route between Colonel Driant's original grave site and Beaumont, and the climb to the top of Wavrille Hill. The nearest cafés and toilets are more than five kilometres away in Vacherauville and you will meet few visitors, so make sure you have everything you need. There are picnic tables under trees by the car park where the tour begins and ends.

Warning: When walking this sector visitors should stay on the paths and keep away from the edges of holes. Do not attempt to enter bunkers or old dugouts. Firing range restrictions apply to this tour so check the dates before you start (see *Advice to Tourers*).

The tour begins in the car park **(1)** close to the memorial to Lieutenant Colonel Emile Driant, which stands by the side of the D905 road from Vacherauville to Ville-devant-Chaumont. Having parked, return to the road junction and take the left fork on the D125. Cross the road to the *Sentier de Découverte* sign and follow the path to Colonel Driant's forward command post. This is a concrete blockhouse known as R2 **(2)**.

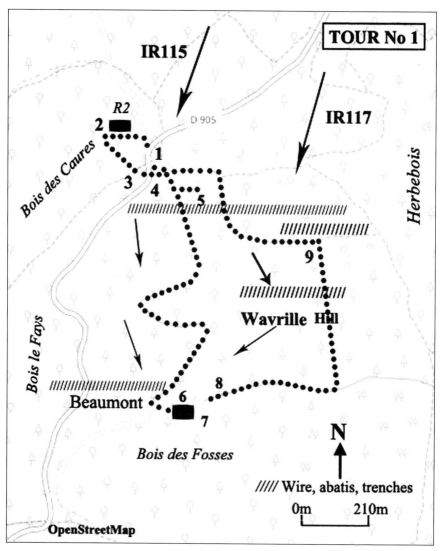

Tour No 1.

There is information in three languages nearby and further information is to be found in my book *Walking Verdun. A Guide to the Battlefield.* Follow the path past the blockhouse and continue through the trenches to Colonel Driant's memorial by the D905 **(3)**. His final burial and this memorial will be described at the end of the tour. Cross the D905 and continue to the small memorial in the clearing ahead **(4)**. Take care when you cross as drivers will not be expecting pedestrians.

2

Colonel Driant's forward command post, known as R2. *Author's collection*

A postcard view of Colonel Driant's memorial. Note the hand at the top of the stone. *Author's collection*

These two memorials commemorate *Lieutenant Colonel Emile Driant*, commander of the 56th and 59th Chasseurs à pied (Light Infantry), who was killed in the late afternoon of 22 February 1916, the second day of the Battle of Verdun. Why should a man who died at such an early stage of the battle and whose troops failed to stem the German tide have two memorials and why is his former command post one of the most famous sites on the battlefield? Who was the man so often referred to as the first hero of Verdun, and why was he important?

Emile Driant was born on September 1855 at Neufchâtel-sur-Aisne, a small town in rural France not far from Rheims. His father was a Justice of the Peace, a small cog in the machinery of local justice but not a military man. At the age of ten Driant entered college in Rheims where, according to his own description, he was a rather turbulent pupil but in the end was sufficiently successful to enter the St. Cyr military academy in 1875. He did not come from a military family, although on his mother's side there were a number of generals and his paternal grandfather had actually seen the great

Colonel Driant. *Author's collection*

Napoleon twice, on one occasion being close enough to reach out and touch his heavy grey greatcoat, still wet with dew after bivouacking among the men. While such memories were enough to inspire any small boy to become a soldier, for Driant the decisive factor in his choice was the traumatic defeat of France at Sedan in the Franco-Prussian war of 1870-1871 and the German annexation of the eastern French provinces of Alsace and Lorraine. Entering St. Cyr in October 1875, Driant graduated two years later in fourth place – no turbulent pupil now – and was posted as a second lieutenant to the 54th Infantry, one of the regiments guarding the new eastern border of France. Here he discovered the fortress system then under construction, and in particular Forts Génicourt and Liouville, which

Second Lieutenant Driant. *Author's collection*

4

The ravelin at Fort Genicourt. *Author's collection*

were important in resisting the German attempt to pinch out Verdun in September 1914.

In the long run, service with the 54th was not really exciting enough for Emile Driant and he applied for a transfer to the 4th Zouaves, an elite regiment stationed in Tunisia. Here, he served under the famous, not to say notorious, General Boulanger, a political general whose popularity was so great that he was regarded as a danger by both the Left and the Right of the political spectrum. Driant's connection with Boulanger, his marriage to the general's daughter, his strong Catholic faith and later the firm and public stand he took against the unlawful collection of data on the religious and political affiliations of army officers, did not enhance his career prospects and, despite receiving ever-more glowing reports from his superior officers, he did not receive the promotion that he was due. In 1905, having already served for ten years as a major and reached the age limit for promotion to lieutenant colonel, Driant resigned from the army. In future if he could not defend France as a soldier, he would do so through writing and politics.

Driant was first and foremost a patriot and seeing the rise of German militarism he feared for France. In 1906, after covering German exercises in Silesia for a French newspaper, he published a little work with the eloquent title of *Vers un nouveau Sedan* [Towards a new Sedan], which set out his views on the military situation and the relative strengths of France and Germany. It caused quite a stir. His patriotism, his gift for argument, his strong feeling of approaching peril, and his willingness to speak out, all led him into politics and in 1910 he entered parliament as the member for Nancy. This was the only major city in Lorraine to remain

The square named after Colonel Driant in Nancy. *Author's collection*

French after 1871. In parliament he served on the Army Commission, where his particular concerns were, unsurprisingly, strengthening national defence and extending national service from two years to three. Unlike many of his contemporaries, Driant understood the need for heavy artillery and increased firepower, and he argued in favour of replacing the Lebel rifle with an automatic rifle. He also turned his attention to the army command structure, right up to the level of commander-in-chief. However, Driant is best remembered for his part in the creation of a new decoration to reward individual acts of valour which could be awarded posthumously: this was the *Croix de Guerre*. The only decorations existing when war broke out were the *Légion d'Honneur* and the *Médaille Militaire* and neither could be awarded after death. (In this case the French were not alone; for example, only the VC could be awarded posthumously to British and Dominion service men – though some instances of awards of lesser decorations certainly push the bounds of the restriction.)

But Emile Driant was not just a politician; he was also a well known writer and journalist. While still in the army he had begun to publish novels under the rather transparent pseudonym of Captain Danrit, and his patriotic sentiments, combined with his professional experience and training, led him naturally towards novels with a military theme. His output was substantial and at the time immensely popular. His approach consisted of giving a military application to the latest scientific inventions and his work was quickly compared to that of Jules Verne. His first work, *La Guerre de Demain* [Tomorrow's War], a cycle of stories dealing with revenge for the French defeat at Sedan in 1870 and the loss of Alsace-Lorraine, took the reader to the forts of eastern France in which he had served as a young officer, and the events he described were not very different from what actually took place when the Germans attacked in 1914. Other novels dealt with submarines, electrified obstacles, airships, vertical take-off planes, helicopters, radio, aircraft carriers, aerial bombardment, chemical and biological weapons, the rise of national trade unions with their international revolutionary and anarchist links, and even modern underground fortresses.

The cover of *L'Aviateur du Pacifique*, with typically exciting illustration. *Author's collection*

To War

With such a background it was not surprising that when war was declared in August 1914 Driant applied for a command, even though his age and his parliamentary seat would have exempted him. His old friend General Foch had promised to take him on the staff if the occasion arose; but in the end he was posted to Verdun, where he took command of the 56th and 59th Battalions of Chasseurs à pied, 72nd Division. They were reservists, generally men of small stature, physically strong and often turbulent, but Driant knew how to handle them and they respected him. Always concerned with keeping up morale and maintaining the cohesion of his two battalions, he immediately supported the idea of a trench newspaper and paid for it to be printed in Paris. *Le Son du Cor* [The Sound of the Horn], first appeared in May 1915 and came out every month until February 1916. He also had a cemetery created for those chasseurs who died on service. It was marked by a cross four metres high and a statue of a young woman imploring God to grant victory in exchange for the lives which had been sacrificed.

In February 1916, Driant's two battalions were holding an advanced position on a strategic hilltop at the northern edge of a large block of woodland generally known as Bois des Caures. The hilltop was strategic because it commanded two roads which ran between the German lines and the Meuse valley. The chasseurs' positions were laid out as a series of separate centres of resistance, backed by a second line of small earth and timber positions and then a third line of concrete redoubts. Driant did

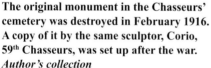

The original monument in the Chasseurs' cemetery was destroyed in February 1916. A copy of it by the same sculptor, Corio, 59th Chasseurs, was set up after the war. *Author's collection*

The copy was destroyed in the Second World War. This modern version was inaugurated in 2016. *Author's collection*

his best to organize the position with the men and materials available but, in August 1915, when General Joffre issued a decree downgrading the status of Verdun from an independent fortress to a mere fortified region and stripped its defences to the bone, he became seriously alarmed. By then he believed Verdun to be too weak to withstand a major offensive and his contacts in diplomatic circles outside France had convinced him that a major offensive would soon be launched in the area.

Driant tried to raise the alarm through normal army channels but his letters were ignored, so in August 1915, using his position as a member of parliament, he wrote directly to the President of the Parliament warning him of the weakness of the front and asking him to pass the information to the Minister for War, General Gallieni. General Joffre was furious but he could not prevent a delegation from the Army Commission

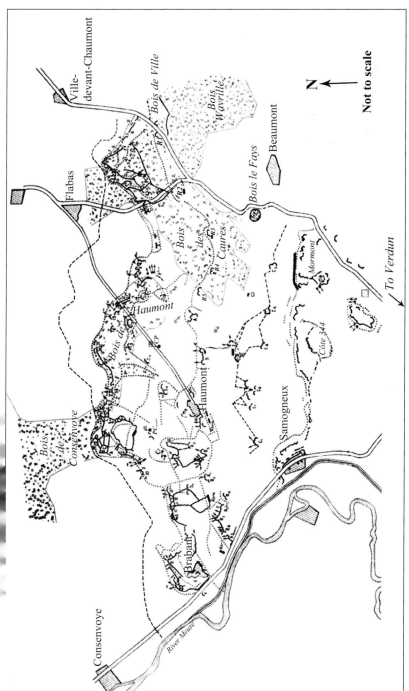

The 72nd Division's positions at the start of the battle. The Chasseurs held the wooded hilltops immediately south of Flabas.

9

from being sent to Verdun to make a report. This was followed in January 1916 by a visit from the Chief of the General Staff, General de Castelnau, who also made a report. Both noted very serious deficiencies but by that time it was too late to do much about it.

General de Castelnau.
Author's collection

When the German bombardment began on 21 February, Driant had approximately 1200 men under his command – two Chasseur battalions and a handful of infantry units forming part of the 72nd Infantry Division. They were supported by six batteries of 75mm field guns and eight heavy batteries. Opposite them were the Hessian 21st and 25th Infantry Divisions, XVIII Corps, eighteen battalions in all, supported by sixty-nine batteries, pioneer, flamethrower and machine gun companies, observation planes, and balloons.

The Chasseurs were expecting them. In two parts of the front French and German front lines were very close together and listening posts had been set up. Earth conduction telegraphy allowed entire conversations to be picked up, including on one occasion detailed orders for small patrols armed with hand grenades to penetrate Bois des Caures in order to seek out the main points of resistance. Other messages identified the German units opposite, their movements, officers, and the improvements being made to the position. All the messages picked up pointed to an increasing number of troops in the sector and preparations for an attack; some referred to the ammunition supply and even gave the percentage of various types of shells to be fired. On 18 February, a drunken German

A concrete observation and small arms post on the roadside close to R2.
Author's collection

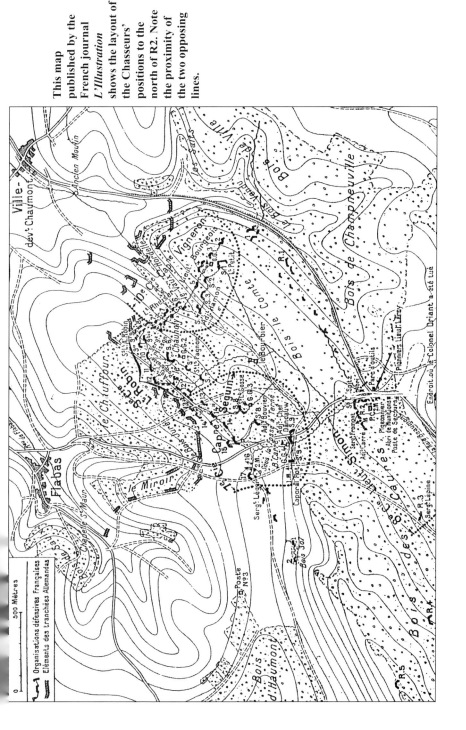

This map published by the French journal *L'Illustration* shows the layout of the Chasseurs' positions to the north of R2. Note the proximity of the two opposing lines.

soldier who lost his way in the dark gave his German speaking interrogator precise details of the coming assault, right down to gun and flamethrower emplacements, troop numbers and even the alcohol ration. 'The attack will be terrible', he said. 'There won't be a blade of grass left; it'll be like nothing you've ever seen before.' Driant had no doubt about what was coming. 'They'll get a bloody nose', he wrote to a friend on 10 February, 'but what will be left of my poor battalions when the cyclone has passed?' The morning of 21 February was particularly beautiful, frosty and sharp, with a clear sky and bright sun. Driant's headquarters were a couple of kilometres behind the lines and at 6am, having handed his wedding ring and other personal objects to his servant with the request that they be returned to his family 'if certain events occurred', he mounted his horse and rode up the crackling forest paths to R2 and walked out into Bois des Caures where his men were already working. While he was talking to them there was a sudden burst of fire. Abbé Adrien Millan (French clergy, like those of most of the other combatants, were liable for conscription), a telephonist with 9 Company, 59th Battalion, remembered that:

> 'At 7am, all was quiet. The runners arrived from the front line with written reports for the company commanders. Nothing special: some noise in the wire, sounds of a pickaxe underground, a car headlight and a bugle down on the Flabas road.'

But that soon changed:

> 'Suddenly, at 7.20am there was a hurricane of fire. We could hear nothing but shells whistling through the air and continuous explosions. It never stopped; a thousand guns firing on targets spotted the previous day by scores of planes flying very low and seeing us clearly. It was like an enormous drum roll with explosions every second. You cannot imagine what it was like!
>   In our little shelter, which was just covered by a few tree trunks and stones and hidden from German eyes by branches and wire, we were shaken by every explosion. It was deafening; it would drive you mad.
>   A 220mm [shell] fell a few metres away. The explosion blew out the candle. Then two more fell just behind the shelter. I lit the candle for the third time because things were getting critical and the lieutenant had ordered me to burn the sector plans and documents if the enemy came.
>   A fourth shell fell, then a fifth and a sixth. They were all round

R2 in November 1915. *Author's collection*

the command post. We had definitely been spotted! I shielded the candle flame to stop it going out but it was a waste of time. The 155s, 210s and 420s had no pity; the air was shaking as much as the ground.'

Trenches and tracks were soon demolished, making it difficult for stretcher bearers to do their work. The chaplain, Abbé de Martimprey, who was also a medical orderly, set off with a stretcher bearer to answer an urgent call from the command post. It was not far, but:

'We had hardly gone 30 metres when the communication trench was blocked by enormous branches. A bit further on we were stopped by a huge shell crater right in the middle of the trench so we had to climb on to the parapet, go around the crater and jump down into the trench again. It was deep in water and did not offer much shelter. The next problem was a whole tree which had fallen full length into the trench. We had to climb out, run as fast as we could, and try to get back into the trench again while all the time shells were falling and exploding around us. It was not long before everything was smashed. There was no trace of the trench and the ground was all churned up; the only thing to do was run for the command post as fast as we could. It was only 50 metres away but we could have been killed a hundred times in that distance; everything was falling down around us.'

13

Like the other units on the quiet northern front at Verdun, the chasseurs had experienced nothing like that level of bombardment and the effect was terrifying. It continued relentlessly until 4pm, when small German patrols began to move forward, expecting to find no resistance. To their astonishment they found determined survivors and there was hand to hand fighting in the wood until night fell.

Although the chasseurs had held their position, Driant knew that the situation was critical. In the centre of his position, where the lines were close together, the Germans had scarcely advanced beyond the outpost line, and a late evening counter attack recovered the lost ground. However, they had carried the sector on the chasseurs' left and were already infiltrating along the ravine on their right where the D905 runs today. During the night Driant visited his lines, saw to the evacuation of the wounded and got the pioneers to carry out makeshift repairs to the

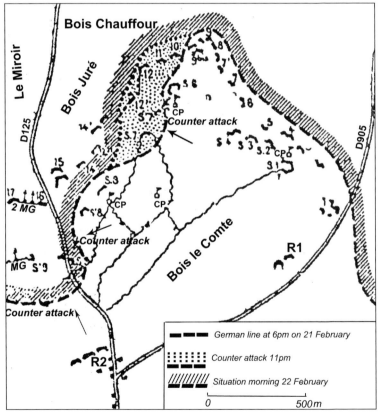

The German assault of 21 February left the Chasseurs holding a narrow salient which could not be defended for long.

14

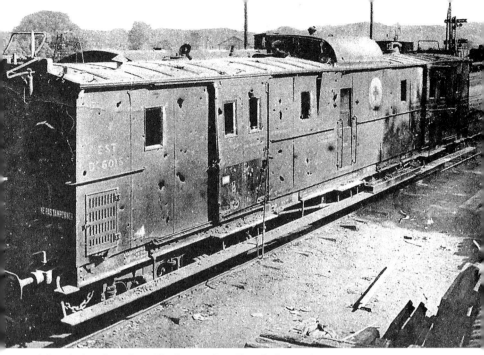

A hospital train waits at Verdun station. *Tom Gudmestad*

command post; but he could offer little comfort. At 7.30am next morning the bombardment began again and at midday large numbers of German troops, preceded by flamethrowers and pioneers, began to push forward on either side of the hilltop. The Chasseurs did what they could to resist but little by little the survivors were pushed back to R2. Driant scribbled a message that they were being attacked by overwhelming numbers and that he was down to his last reserves, and then rallied his men and deployed them on either side of the command post. They were able to hold the Germans off for a while but by mid afternoon they were in danger of being cut off. The choice was now to die where they stood or to withdraw to the French second line and live to fight another day. Despite the urgency of the situation, Driant called his remaining officers together to discuss the matter and finally ordered withdrawal. Unhurriedly, he collected his sheepskin jacket, visited the first aid post by the road to reassure the injured that they would be properly looked after and then, with the scattered remnants of his command, he set off towards the second line.

Driant's death
To continue the tour, cross the D905 and follow the *Sentier du Bois des Caures* to the memorial in the clearing a short distance ahead **(4)**.

By the time Driant and his men were withdrawing the Germans had reached the edge of the wood and the open ground ahead of the chasseurs was swept with fire. Driant stopped to offer first aid to one of his men and then, shaking hands with him, stood up and was hit in the head. From his prisoner of war camp Sergeant Jules Hacquin, 59th Chasseurs, described what he saw then:

'I had just scrambled into a shell hole when a sergeant, who was accompanying Colonel Driant and was a couple of steps ahead of him, jumped in on top of me. After he jumped in, I clearly saw the colonel right on the edge of our shell hole throw out his arms with a cry and crumple up. There were such mounds of earth around our hole that we could not see him once he had fallen but we realized that he had been wounded and, using our hands, we tried to dig away the earth that blocked our view. We wanted to pull him close to us without getting out of the shell hole. As soon as we had dug enough to see him, it was clear there were no signs of life. Blood was running from his head and his mouth, his eyes were half closed and he was deathly pale.'

The little memorial, which looks rather like a section of low wall, marks the spot where Colonel Driant is believed to have died. The slightly mystifying inscription *'Ils sont tombés silencieux sous le choc comme une muraille'* [As a wall they fell, silent under the onslaught] is a reference to the 1845 battle of Sidi Brahim in which a combined force of almost five hundred hussars and chasseurs was attacked by Berber troops in what was then French Algeria. Only eleven men survived the encounter and a French column passing the site five months later found the dead still lying where they had fallen 'like an old wall that had been breached'. Their remains were reverently gathered together for burial before being transferred to the Chasseurs museum at Vincennes, near Paris, where they remain. One of the few survivors of that battle was the bugler, Guillaume Rolland, who in 1913 at the age of ninety two was named an Officer of the Legion of Honour at a ceremony attended by Colonel Driant. In his honour, Driant named one of the Chasseurs' camps in the rear of these lines *Camp Rolland*. The battle of Sidi Brahim is still commemorated each year by the Chasseurs and the annual ceremony held at Driant's roadside memorial on the Sunday closest to 21 February is known locally by that name.

With the memorial behind you, continue to the sign reading *Tombe Provisoire du Colonel Driant 350m*; turn right and continue to the next

The memorial marks the spot where Colonel Driant is believed to have died.
Author's collection

sign, then turn left into the wood to visit the site of Colonel Driant's original grave **(5)**.

Burial by the Germans
None of the one hundred or so chasseurs who made it back to French lines had any definite news of Colonel Driant and it was some days before rumours of his death reached Paris. It was the King of Spain, an old friend of the family, who asked the Germans for information. The first firm news, received in April, referred to the burial of both Colonel Driant and Major Renouard, commander of the 59th Chasseurs, and included map references.

Major Renouard, commander of the 59th Battalion of Chasseurs. *Author's collection*

Some months later a German baroness, whose son had found the colonel's body, wrote to Madame Driant, informing her that her husband had been buried with honour and that his grave would be tended until peace returned. She also offered to return an engraved medallion which Driant had worn.

On 3 November 1918 a French reconnaissance party reached the site and found it to be as described. Crosses had been placed at the head of the graves, which had been carefully outlined with stones. The reconnaissance party identified the site and replaced the two crosses, tidying up the area, which had been slightly damaged by recent shelling, but not opening the graves. It was not until 9 August 1919 that the bodies

The German graves of Colonel Driant and Major Renouard. *Author's collection*

were exhumed in the presence, among others, of Madame Driant, General Renouard (the Major's father) and the military governor of Verdun. Colonel Driant's body was identified by the braid on his uniform and by a wedding ring in his pocket, which belonged to one of his lieutenants, Henri Petitcollot, a mining engineer in civilian life, who had asked the colonel to return it to his wife if he did not survive. Petitcollot was wounded on 21 February and died at an evacuation hospital the following day. Thirty nine year old Major Renouard, a highly decorated staff officer who had recently been seconded to the chasseurs for front line experience, had also been killed in the withdrawal. His body was removed for provisional burial in the Faubourg Pavé military cemetery in Verdun, while Colonel Driant's remains were placed in a coffin and reburied at the same site until a permanent resting place had been found. The story of the events leading up to his final burial at the memorial by the roadside will be told at the end of the tour.

A postcard view of Colonel Driant's grave after identification and reburial in November 1918. *Author's collection*

Colonel Driant's grave as it was until recently and as it is now. *Author's collection*

Until a few years ago this site was marked by a rough outline of stones and the type of cross used in French military cemeteries but recent refurbishment has modernized its appearance.

On to Beaumont
To continue the tour, return to the main path, turn left and continue along the *Sentier du Bois des Caures* until you reach Beaumont (roughly two kilometres).

The two infantry divisions meeting the German assault on 21 February 1916 were the 72nd and 51st, with the current D905 forming the divisional boundary. The next part of the tour covers sectors defended by the 51st Division.

20

Like the advanced position, the second position was also based on villages, hilltops and forests, and it included Beaumont, a small but solid cluster of terraced houses and farms built along one street with a population in 1911 of 186. Over the centuries Beaumont had suffered plenty of disruption, including three invasions and two cholera epidemics, but in the nineteenth century agricultural developments had brought prosperity and a short lived population increase, while the development of the fortress system around Verdun brought contact with men from other parts of France. As a result, shopkeepers prospered, ideas changed and some of the old ways of life disappeared, to the sorrow of some of the more traditional inhabitants. However, all that came to an end with the outbreak of war. In September 1914, with the Germans only a few kilometres to the north, the population was evacuated. The houses were turned into strong redoubts, fronted by terraces of trenches and defended by thick belts of wire, which by the time the Germans attacked stretched from the village right across the D905 to the southern edge of Bois des Caures.

Beaumont, and Bois des Fosses, which lay behind it, were the 25th Division's intended objectives; but by the time the Hessians emerged from the thick woods that they had been fighting through all day darkness was falling, their left flank was in the air and a thundering barrage was smashing into the edge of Bois des Caures and making it impossible to break out. Unable to advance, the Hessians prepared to spend a second freezing night in the open. Despite the overwhelming difference in resources between attackers and defenders, the day had not been as successful as German commanders had hoped. The 25th Division had already lost almost 300 men and there was no question of trying to advance until German artillery could deal with the problems that lay ahead.

The main street of Beaumont before the battle. *Author's collection*

A battery of French 155mm guns that has seen better days. *Author's collection*

The forest cover in this area today makes it impossible to see what lay ahead of the Hessians when dawn broke on 23 February 1916. The task of taking Beaumont had fallen to Infantry Regiment 115 (25th Division) and facing them was a wide corridor of bare ground roughly 1500 metres long, narrow at the top and widening out as it reached the entrenched guns in front of Beaumont. The entrance to the corridor was blocked by a whole series of obstacles, beginning with an abatis – felled trees placed lengthwise over each other with the boughs pointing outwards – backed by wire entanglements and deep trenches with traverses and fire bays. The corridor was commanded on the right by Bois Le Fays, a small wood stuffed with guns covering a steep slope on the western side of the D905, on the left by Wavrille, a roughly pear shaped hill, approximately one kilometre long, wooded, entrenched, and almost entirely surrounded by wire. Batteries to the south of Beaumont also had the attackers in their sights.

It was clear to German commanders that without support a frontal attack on Beaumont would be suicidal, so another Hessian regiment, the 117th, was ordered to help clear the guns from the western side of Wavrille before breaking out and assisting in the assault. The remainder of the hill was to be cleared by Leib-Grenadier Regiment 8, an elite Brandenburg regiment from the 5th Division. It was not an inviting prospect. Wavrille was the highest point in the area and the sweeping views offered by the summit made it an important link in the chain of second line defences. For several days men had been involved in deepening trenches and extending wire between Wavrille and the positions on either side. There were infantry and machine gunners throughout the wood; but the strongest French positions were along the northern edge and across the summit. Losing Wavrille would allow the Germans to outflank Beaumont and the commander of XXX Corps, General Chrétien, had ordered it to be held at all costs.

Defence of Beaumont: 21 – 22 February
Beaumont was defended by the 327th Infantry, a reserve regiment from northern France whose two battalions were split between three sectors: the village, Wavrille, and the ridges and ravines of Bois des Fosses some 500 metres to the south. Despite fierce cold, and for those on Wavrille and in the wood a total lack of shelter, the 327th had worked for days to improve existing defences and develop new ones. Trenches were deepened, camouflaged and in some places doubled, dug outs were excavated, wire extended and centres of resistance linked by communication trenches. On 21 February the whole area came under

Going up to the line with picks and shovels. *Author's collection*

23

heavy bombardment; casualties mounted, rations failed to get through and the horses had to be evacuated, which meant that guns and field kitchens had later to be abandoned to the enemy. The following day the 327th was reinforced by four companies of the 208th Infantry, another reserve regiment from northern France. While two companies joined the garrison of the village, two others took up position at the edge of Bois des Fosses. The bombardment was intense and French guns appeared not to be responding. Sending a runner to the nearest battery did not help, nor did the battalion commander's urgent request for an artillery officer to be sent to Beaumont with a telephone link to the nearest battery and a supply of signal rockets.

23 February: Wavrille Hill
The third day of the German offensive opened with another shattering bombardment and at 12.30pm the Hessians moved off. On the right, two companies of Infantry Regiment 115 advanced towards Beaumont in close lines as if on the parade ground. All was quiet; not a shot was fired for 300 metres but, just as Wavrille Hill came into view, French guns opened up from all sides and waves of fire tore into the packed ranks, mowing the attackers down. German artillery furiously targeted the batteries that were blasting shells into the 115th but they failed to put them out of action and after several hours of desperate effort, with no let up in the French bombardment and the ground too frozen to dig in, the assault was called off.

By that time Wavrille Hill had fallen. There were French infantry and machine gunners all over the hill but the strongest defences were along the northern and western sides. Here, the defenders, basically elements of the 327th and 310th Infantry Regiments, now swelled by survivors from other parts of the line, had been stunned by a devastating bombardment by trench mortars and heavy howitzers, including the 420mm giant known as 'Big Bertha'. There had already been several unsuccessful attempts to capture the hill, including a daring assault launched in pitch darkness at 4am that morning; but later, following a bombardment of even more terrifying intensity, the Leib-Grenadiers finally broke through the northern defences and pushed the French right off the hill. Only a handful of men managed to escape, all in the last stages of exhaustion. At the same time a small mixed group from Infantry Regiments 117 and 115 attacked the western edge of the hill, captured nine machine guns and removed the danger of flanking fire but were too late to do any more that day. It had been a bloody day for both sides. The attack on Wavrille Hill had cost the Leib-Grenadiers and Infantry Regiment 117 over four hundred officers and men, while the disastrous

The 42cm howitzer nicknamed 'Big Bertha'. *Author's collection*

frontal assault on Beaumont by Infantry Regiment 115 had added 300 more names to a casualty list already touching 600. As for the defenders, Beaumont and Wavrille Hill had cost the 327th almost four hundred and fifty officers and men and there was worse to come.

That night the temperature sank to -6C. "Cold enough to freeze you solid", was the verdict of one French corporal and it was no better for the Germans. There was no hot food for either side.

During the night Infantry Regiment 115 was withdrawn, unable to do more. The 117th took over and on 24 February they managed to push the line forward, overrunning the French positions in front of the village and capturing abandoned guns, limbers and – to their delight – the field kitchens which, without horses, could not be withdrawn in time. By now they were now quite close to Beaumont but the advance had left them in an open salient which was still commanded by the guns in Bois Le Fays. It was a terrible position but there was a glimmer of hope: during the day Bois Le Fays had been outflanked. Once it fell, the Germans would be able to fire directly down into Beaumont and the village would be lost.

Zouaves in the woods close to Bois Le Fays. *Author's collection*

24 February 1916: Beaumont falls

The softening up process began early and for hours huge 210mm and 305mm shells came crashing down on Beaumont and surrounding positions. At around 10am, having tried unsuccessfully to outflank Beaumont along the valley where the D905 runs today, massed ranks of Germans preceded by hand grenade units appeared to the north of the village, advancing almost without firing a shot. Desperate rocket signals from the village brought no response; but machine guns in Bois Le Fays firing straight into the oncoming mass brought men down in whole ranks and the survivors ran for shelter, leaving the ground covered with heaps of wounded and dying men. A second attempt brought the same result.

However, with Wavrille Hill in German hands it was only a matter of time until the village fell and at around 1pm observers in Bois Le Fays saw German soldiers pushing into Beaumont from the eastern side. They were closely followed by others coming from the north. The defenders managed to contain the assault for a while, and there was bitter fighting around the French command post in the church; but in the end they could not prevent the Germans from steadily working their way through the village and hauling men out of dugouts and cellars. There were no more messages from Beaumont after 1.30pm and Bois Le Fays was evacuated

**Beaumont church before
complete destruction.**
Author's collection

**French prisoners under
guard.** *Wim Degrande*

some hours later. Almost 700 officers and men fell in the final day's
defence of the village, adding to the almost 1300 casualties suffered since
the start of the offensive four days earlier.

Beaumont remained in German hands until almost the end of the war.
The limited offensive launched by the French in August 1917 failed to

retake the village, despite overwhelming material superiority. It was finally recaptured by elements of the French 26th Division during the Franco-American Meuse-Argonne offensive (see below on the recapture of Wavrille Hill).

The destroyed village
For information about the decision not to rebuild Beaumont and a number of other destroyed villages, see the chapter entitled *Aftermath* and the information boards by the church. When you reach the site of the village, turn uphill along the former main street. The chapel **(6)**, built in 1933 and dedicated to Saint Maurice, stands on the site of the former church. Continue past the chapel to the walled cemetery **(7)** and note the damaged well head on the right, which is the only remnant of the original village.

The modern chapel at Beaumont. *Author's collection*

The well head, the only remnant of the old village. *Author's collection*

The war memorial at Beaumont, inaugurated in 1925. *Author's collection*

The Cemetery
1st Gunner/Driver [Canonnier/Conducteur] Julian Quenet, 61st Field
Artillery
Even though Beaumont was not rebuilt, the sons of the village were not
forgotten. The cemetery was cleared and refurbished, and in 1925 a war
memorial was erected bearing Beaumont's citation in Army Orders and
an alphabetical list of the sixteen men who died for France. This was a

**Recent refurbishment of Julien Quenet's grave has
replaced the earlier simple memorial with a
handsome stone.**

29

devastating number in so small a place, especially as five of them came from only two families. Thirty eight year old Julien Quenet, whose family was living in Beaumont before the French Revolution, died of wounds at the field hospital at Bras-sur-Meuse in November 1915; he is the only son of the village to have returned to his ancestral home. It was another Quenet, mayor of the destroyed village for many years after the war, who was responsible for building the chapel and the war memorial. The memorial inscription on his gravestone reads 'He died so that France should stand'.

Sergeant Charles Flipo, 208th Infantry
On each side of the entrance gate there are memorials to men who are not the sons of Beaumont. Charles Flipo, a sergeant in 18 Company, 208th Infantry, was a textile worker from Tourcoing when he was mobilized. Although a reserve regiment, the 208th had seen serious action from the beginning of the war, including at Dinant, Guise, the first Battle of the Marne, and the first and second Battles of Champagne. The early weeks of 1916 saw the 208th developing and improving defences in various sectors at Verdun, and when the German offensive began Charles Flipo was quartered in Fort Douaumont. The next day his regiment was ordered to Bois des Fosses and, in a bombardment so intense that they could barely get forward, Flipo and his comrades dug in close to Beaumont. Corporal Edouard Bougard, 208th Infantry, described the rush to get there:

'We ran like madmen to get to Beaumont where we had to support a battalion of the 327th. We had to lift up the wire to get underneath it and that held us up. We scrambled over corpses, puffing and panting in our fever to get forward. The ravine was completely churned up by shells, nothing but enormous craters, six or ten metres across. As we were racing forward, a huge shell suddenly fell right on the company's First Section. Ten men wounded and fifteen killed by that one shell, all blown up... flesh and blood rained down on us. The noise was infernal. Huge trees in Bois des Fosses, as wide as wine barrels, were flying into the air, chopped up like bits of straw.'

It was a violent onslaught and when it ended 18 Company had suffered eighty four casualties; they included thirty two year old Sergeant Flipo, who had been wounded for the third time. Two days later he was listed as dead and his body was never found. Although the memorial and his death certificate give him the rank of sergeant, the war diaries of both the

327th and 208th Infantry Regiments make him a lieutenant. A married man with several children, Charles Flipo is also remembered on the war memorial in Tourcoing. Tiberghien was his wife's maiden name.

Private Henri Michelet, 154th Infantry
Twenty-one year old Private Henri Michelet also disappeared without trace, although this time it was in 1917. Born in Vaucouleurs, some seventy kilometres south of Verdun, he joined the 155th Infantry but later transferred to its sister regiment, the 154th. During the French offensive of August 1917 the 154th was facing Bois Le Fays, while the 155th was facing the village. At 4.45am both regiments moved off as planned but they ran into a violent bombardment of gas and high explosive, supported by machine guns firing from the ruins of the village. The 154th's war diary only mentions 'numerous losses' and nothing is known of the last hours of Private Michelet's life. He is remembered on the war memorial at Vaucouleurs and by the plaque placed here by his family in 2008.

The handsome memorial to Charles Flipo. *Author's collection*

Henri Michel disappeared without trace but he has not been forgotten by his family. *Author's collection*

Erwin Müller
From the cemetery, turn right uphill. Pass the green and white painted barrier and walk ahead. Where the track forks, ignore the left fork and keep straight on for a short distance until you reach the damaged memorial to Erwin Müller, which stands in undergrowth on the left **(8)**. This is a rare survival of the Battle of Verdun and it is unfortunate that the inscription is too damaged to read. The date appears to be November 1916, but the combination of damage and a common German name has so far made it impossible to find out more. Leaving the memorial on your left continue ahead along the track, which is likely to remain **extremely wet**. In 1916 this was open country; the northern edge of Bois des Fosses was some 500 metres to your right, while the wooded edge of Wavrille Hill was directly ahead. After approximately 750 metres you will reach Cote 351, a high point that the French were ordered to defend to the last man in

February 1916. Four tracks join here. Ignore the track running diagonally left and turn straight uphill with block 170 on the right and 164 on the left. The track rises to the summit of the hill. It was heavily shelled in 1917 and is likely to be wet all year.

Wavrille Hill

When the German offensive began in February 1916 most of Wavrille Hill was forested but a clearing on the hilltop provided commanding views and made it a key defensive position. During the German occupation observers and signallers from many different regiments were stationed here. While Fort Douaumont was in German hands one particularly important signalling station, a link in the chain of signalling posts to the rear, was in constant contact with the receiving

Not many German memorials survived battlefield clearance. This is one of the few that did. *Author's collection*

station in the fort's 75mm gun turret. For more information about the gun turret and Fort Douaumont, see my book *Verdun: Fort Douaumont*. Stop when you reach the highest point on the track.

A signalling station on the top of Wavrille Hill. *Author's collection*

Two of the many bunkers on Wavrille Hill. *Author's collection*

Some of the bunkers in this area are named. This one is *Seehund* **(sea lion).** *Jan Carel Broek Roelofs*

For most of 1916 Wavrille Hill was several kilometres behind the front and, apart from observation and signalling, it played no great part in the battle. However, that changed in December 1916, when a successful French counter offensive brought the front to within three kilometres of where you are now standing. To reinforce this area a strong defensive line known as the *Brabanter-Stellung* was constructed, comprising machine guns, pickets and advanced sentry posts, as well as a substantial number of concrete bunkers on the top of the hill; and also *Stollenkaserne*, deep underground barracks that offered shelter from bombardment. While these were good in theory, in practice being underground was far from pleasant. As soon as shells started to fall everyone, whether from Wavrille Hill or the surrounding areas and regardless of whether or not they were entitled to do so, raced for the barracks and flung themselves inside. Men who needed to get out quickly, such as runners, signallers, stretcher bearers and men from other regiments, hogged the stairs and made it difficult for other men to get in or out. The only ventilation was provided

Officers inspect a deep excavation for a bunker. *Tom Gudmestad*

by hand operated fans that stood outside the barracks, which meant they could not be worked during a bombardment. So many men in so small a space made the air hot and thick; candles and lamps burned low and if, as sometimes happened, the press of men inside overturned a latrine barrel, conditions quickly became unbearable. Irritable, apathetic, hot, hungry and thirsty, men pressed against one another inside the hot, dark rooms, tried to avoid being trodden on and waited for the moment they could get outside again. At times like that, officers had great difficulty keeping their men calm and together.

1918: Beaumont and Wavrille Hill recaptured

On 8 October 1918 units of the French 26th Infantry Division, operating under American command, attacked Beaumont and Wavrille Hill as part of a general offensive in this sector. Supported by a massive artillery bombardment, the assault troops moved off at 5am and little more than three hours later Beaumont was in French hands. At the same time a mixed force of infantry and Senegalese tirailleurs attacked Wavrille Hill with the aim of seizing the observation posts on the top. The defenders – Infantry Regiment 160 – were not prepared to abandon so important a position and it was several hours before the attackers managed to reach the top; and when they did, violent artillery and machine-gun fire, coupled with energetic resistance, prevented them from going any further. The next day was foggy but if the Germans expected it to be quiet they were disappointed, and a furious bombardment was followed by a mass French assault in which Wavrille Hill was outflanked. Somehow German officers managed to scrape together enough men and machine guns to resist but they were too weak to hold out for long and later that day a second assault cleared the hill completely.

A group of German prisoners. *Author's collection*

Stay on the track and continue directly ahead over the hilltop. Most of the bunkers are in block 163 and difficult to see from the track; but as you approach the bottom of the hill there is one visible some fifty metres

35

Another sturdy bunker, although not finished as carefully as Seehund. *Author's collection*

to the left **(9)**. The inscription on the side facing the path refers to the 2. Kompanie Lothringische (Festungs-) Pionier-Bataillon Nr. 20, which built this and other positions here in 1917. When you reach the T-junction with a hard, white road, turn right and follow it back to the car park, then cross the road to the roadside memorial to Colonel Driant.

The roadside memorial

The enormous fame that Colonel Driant had enjoyed before the war only increased as knowledge spread of the chasseurs' desperate stand in the first two days of the battle. The idea of small groups of men, already stunned by a bombardment of unheard of violence, drawing on every reserve to fight on as the grey tide engulfed them, caught the popular imagination, and after the war came the idea that so valiant a stand deserved a special memorial. A local landowner offered a site for the memorial, a committee was put together to raise the funds and a public subscription of 30,000 francs – a very substantial sum in those days –

was opened. The choice of the site aroused a certain amount of ire among the chasseurs as it lay outside their sector and Colonel Driant had always wished to be buried with the chasseurs in Vacherauville, but the plans went ahead and a well-known sculptor was commissioned to create a suitable memorial. Behind the top of the main cross the sun rises and – now too weathered to make out – a hand raised to the sky traces the words which became the motto of the Battle of Verdun *On ne passe pas* [They shall not pass]. Driant's fallen chasseurs are represented by the multitude of smaller crosses rising from the foot of the memorial and by the hunting horn.

On 9 October 1922, Colonel Driant's remains were exhumed for the second time and again formally identified and placed in a coffin that was carried to the nearby village of Ville-devant-Chaumont. The whole village turned out to honour its arrival. The coffin remained in the chapel until 21 October when, in the presence of Madame Driant and numerous dignitaries, Emile Driant was laid to rest. The memorial was inaugurated the next day in a ceremony attended by religious leaders, senior military officers, members of the government, chasseur representatives and the general public in vast numbers. Eight years later, crowds once again trod the muddy paths to Bois des Caures for the inauguration of command post R2 as a museum. There were speeches, a march past by former

This view of children bringing flowers to Colonel Driant's grave became a popular postcard. *Author's collection*

The ceremony to commemorate Colonel Driant is held each year on the Sunday closest to 21 February. It attracts hundreds of people. *Author's collection*

chasseurs, a fly past with aerial acrobatics, and finally a huge banquet in Verdun. It was a testament to the affection and respect in which Lieutenant Colonel Emile Driant was held.

An enormously popular and famous man with a deep love of France, Driant had protested strongly at what he saw as the weakness of the Verdun front and the danger that it represented. That he made himself unpopular at the highest military level did not discourage him from doing what he saw as his duty; and with his men he died for France. For many people after the war, Driant and his chasseurs represented what became known as the 'Verdun phenomenon': men, singly or in small groups, often without officers, fighting on in smashed positions without hope of reinforcement until food and ammunition ran out, determined to do their duty or die where they stood. Considering that it took some elements of XVIII Corps four days of hard fighting to reach the objectives originally set for the second day of the assault, they certainly succeeded.

Colonel Driant is also remembered in Neufchâtel-sur-Aisne, his place of birth. *Author's collection*

38

GPS Waypoints Tour No. 1

1. N49°16.332' E005°24.348'
2. N49°16.333' E005°24.348'
3. N49°16.285' E005°24.333'
4. N49°16.247' E005°24.496'
5. N49°16.191' E005°24.570'
6. N49°15.510' E005°24.419'
7. N49°15.577' E005°25.367'
8. N49°15.549' E005°24.699'
9. N49°16.000' E005°25.276'

Tour No. 2

21–23 February 1916

Azannes-et Soumazannes, Herbebois, Chemin St. André

Distance: Approximately ten kilometres
Duration: A half day's tour
Maps: IGN 3112ET or IGN Blue Series 3112 Ouest.

Circular tour from Azannes-et-Soumazannes to Herbebois, returning via the Chemin St. André.

Memorials on this tour: Offizierstellverträter Otto Drähn, Leutnant Jürgen Freiherr von Eynatten, Vizefeldwebel Otto Schneidereit, Leutnant der Reserve Bernhard Stollbrock, Gefreiter Frantz Maréchal, Unteroffizier Ernst Besecke, Gefreiter der Reserve Johannes Kehlenbach, Kriegsfreiwilliger Paul Weilenmann and Kriegsfreiwilliger Wilhelm Wirtz.

Reaching Herbebois involves two uphill stretches of roughly 1300 metres and 750 metres. The track down into the *Ravin des Renards* is steep but the remainder of the route is reasonably level. Once you leave Azannes-et-Soumazannes there are no cafés or toilets and you are unlikely to meet other visitors, so make sure you have everything you need.

Warning: When walking this sector visitors should stay on the paths and keep away from the edges of holes. Do not attempt to enter any concrete structures or dugouts. Firing range restrictions apply, so check the dates before you start.

The tour begins at the war memorial by the church of St. André in Azannes-et-Soumazannes (1), a small village lying some seventeen kilometres north east of Verdun on the D65. Before the First World War Azannes and Soumazannes were separate places, the latter being a tiny hamlet a short distance away that no longer exists. The war memorial lists the names of nineteen men from both villages who died for France

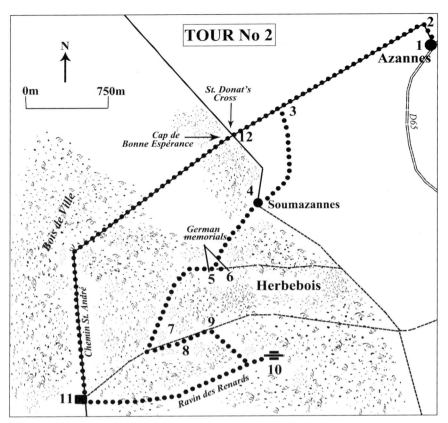

Tour No 2.

Azannes church
during the war.
Wim Degrande

during the First World War, and eleven civilians, including two women,
who died in captivity. Two more names were added during the Second
World War.

With the church on the right, follow the Rue Haute uphill, keeping to
the right at the road fork. Pass the grotto and shrine on the left and keep
straight on uphill to the decorated Gothic gateway. Before the war this

41

German troops in the Rue Haute. *Tony Noyes*

was the entrance to the village cemetery and, together with a handful of old gravestones, it is all that remains of pre-war Azannes.

Azannes I German cemetery
The entrance to Azannes I German cemetery **(2)** is next to the gateway. During the war this small village was a major logistics and supply centre for the Germans, and once the Battle of Verdun began it also became an important medical centre, with several hospitals and other medical services established here. Although this cemetery was created in 1915, most of the 811 men buried here died during the first three months of the Battle of Verdun and they include many who took part in the assault on Fort Douaumont on 25 February 1916. The difficulties of transporting bodies back from the front meant that most men were buried where they fell, and the men buried here had returned from the battlefield wounded and died later. Their regiments represent nearly all parts of the Germany of 1916: Bavaria, Hesse, Saxony, Brandenburg, East Prussia, Mecklenburg, Posen and Holstein.

The only remaining original gravestone is that of Locomotive Driver Friedrich Krell, who fell in Bois des Fosses on 30 April 1916, where his grave was found after the war; his remains were exhumed and reburied in Block 1, Grave 482. The striking memorial on higher ground in the centre of the cemetery commemorates the *Königlichebayerische*

42

The burial of Lieutenant Hans Itzel, Infantry Regiment 117, who died at Douaumont on 21 April 1916. *Wim Degrande*

The family death card for stretcher bearer Ludwig Ammer, 14th Bavarian Stretcher Bearer Company, 14th Infantry Division, who died in shelling on 6 September 1916. He is buried in Block 1, Grave 82. *Wim Degrande*

Friedrich Krell's original gravestone, found in Bois des Fosses after the war. *Author's collection*

The handsome memorial to Königlichebayerische Armierungsbataillion X, a fortunate survivor of the war. *Author's collection*

Armierungsbataillion X (fortification troops), most of whom are buried elsewhere. Beneath the inscription *Getreu bis zum Tode* [Faithful unto Death], an oak crowned Bavarian helmet of the type worn before 1871 surmounts an altar dedicated to the battalion's unforgettable and valiant comrades.

The exhumation of German cemeteries and scattered field graves by French authorities after the war increased the size of this wartime cemetery, and as late as the 1930s German remains were still being transferred here. Today, Azannes I and the larger Azannes II cemetery, which stands a short distance away on the D66 road to Mangiennes, are both maintained by the German war graves authority.

To continue the tour, return through the Gothic gateway, turn right for a few metres and then turn left uphill for one kilometre. Where the track forks and there is a small sign in the hedge pointing left to Soumazannes **(3)**, **stop** and look back over the Woëvre plain.

The Germans had been established on the plain since autumn 1914. The extensive forests, which existed at the time, provided camouflage and shelter for camps, batteries, stations, medical services, workshops and anything else needed, as well as wood, which was consumed in enormous quantities. The rear slopes of the three prominent hills on the skyline to your left offered shelter for numerous German camps and artillery batteries, while the hilltops provided observatories. Now turn and look directly ahead. The hill in front of you is the surprisingly named *Cap de Bonne Espérance* [Cape of Good Hope] and was not wooded at the time. On this side, out of sight of French observers on the hills beyond, there were camps, ammunition and supply dumps and an important dressing station.

German troop shelters. *Landesarchiv Karlsruhe 456 F 106 Nr. 19, Bild 7*

In the weeks prior to the start of the offensive, German pioneers worked flat out to excavate deep mined dugouts and create trench mortar and battery positions on the *Cap de Bonne Espérance*. It was there that infantry, pioneers and gunners huddled from 12 – 21 February, waiting for the offensive to begin. As the rain poured down, water filled the dugouts, pumps were brought up, food went mouldy and rats were everywhere. Shells, lugged forward and piled up in the dark at the cost of much bruising and cursing, sank in the mud; ammunition wagons got stuck and anyone who tried to push them out lost boots, stockings and trousers in the sticky slime. Men were sodden, hungry, exhausted from nightly labouring, miserable from trying to sleep in cramped conditions and wet clothes and, unsurprisingly, many fell ill. It was forbidden to go

A German position under the road from Azannes to the Cap de Bonne Espérance. *Landesarchiv Karlsruhe 456 F 106 Nr. 18, Bild 3*

outside the dugouts during the day and inside, packed like herrings in a barrel, tempers frayed as men waited for the longed for change in the weather. Complaints about the conditions only brought the response that it was temporary; but for the men in the dugouts it was interminable. Despite the misery, the work went on. As the days passed, steps were cut in the parapets, ladders were positioned, gaps were cut in the wire and guns were zeroed in. Patrols went out, one particularly lucky one bringing in a prisoner with useful information. But it kept on raining and, as the water rose, men's spirits fell until no one believed that the offensive would ever begin.

Herbebois
Now take the left fork downhill, following the sign to Soumazannes and **stop** when the fishponds come into view. The wooded massif directly ahead is Herbebois, which was the focus of the 6th Division's assault on 21 February 1916. At that time there were trees on the top of the hill but the lower slopes were bare.

In 1916 Herbebois measured some two kilometres from north to south and slightly less from east to west, and it offered views far and wide. One of the main centres of resistance on the Right Bank of the River Meuse and therefore of great importance, it was separated from the neighbouring centres of Ornes and Bois de Ville by wide gaps defended by wire, flanking fire and trenches. French troops had been there since autumn 1914 and they had used their time to develop defences that included a thick belt of wire in front of the advanced line, another belt 200 metres into the wood fronting the main line of resistance, and a third line behind more wire some 800 metres further back. Dense, dark, thick with undergrowth that prevented passage except through defended gaps, and protected by blockhouses, machine guns and carefully constructed abatis, interlaced with wire and overgrown with thorns and brambles, Herbebois would not be an easy nut to crack.

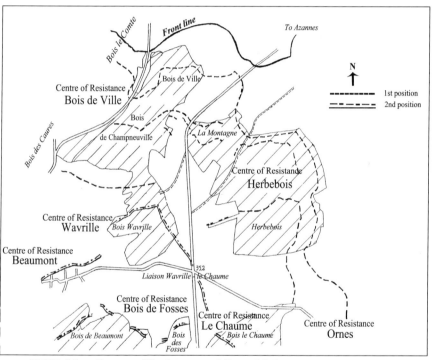

51st Division. Centres of Resistance and lines of defence.

Soumazannes

Continue downhill, pass the entrance to the private fishponds and **stop** when you reach the memorial to Soumazannes **(4)**. In August 1914 this tiny hamlet comprised a handful of houses, a mill, a substantial farm known as the 'Chateau' and a population of thirty. Five men were mobilized and three weeks later the remaining inhabitants fled before the

The memorial to the destroyed village of Soumazannes. *Author's collection*

The 'Chateau' at Soumazannes. *H.P von Müller's Estate*

advancing Germans, leaving Soumazannes between the lines and visited by French and German patrols. From 21 February 1916 to 11 November 1918 the hamlet was in German hands and such was the level of destruction that after the war it became part of the Red Zone. This was the name given to former battle areas expropriated by the government because they could not be restored to pre-war use without excessive expense. The mill, which stood outside the Red Zone, was rebuilt, while any other usable materials were taken away to rebuild Azannes. At the end of the 1920s the government withdrew Soumazannes from the Red

Zone and sold off much of the expropriated land; but the village was still not rebuilt. Of the five men who went to war from Soumazannes, four returned; the only casualty was twenty two year old Louis Louppe, a gunner with the 29th Field Artillery, who was killed to the southeast of Verdun in January 1916. He is commemorated on the war memorial at Azannes and on a stained glass window inside the church.

Now follow the track, which rises steeply into open ground. Continue uphill to the firing range sign, then **stop** and look to your right. While most of the French advanced line ran just inside Herbebois, one part of it left the shelter of the trees and ran diagonally across the hillside to your right before bending sharply and linking up with the French positions on the other side of the ridge. The Germans called this trench the Knochgraben; on 21 February 1916 it was the first objective of one of their most famous regiments, Infantry Regiment 24, whose only fault, at least according to Blücher, was that it was too brave. To reach the Knochgraben the 24th would have to cross several hundred metres of bare ground in full view of Herbebois. However, that was considerably less than the 1000 metres of bare ground which, on your left, Infantry Regiment 64 would have to cover from Soumazannes to reach their first objective. The difference in distance was a headache for the 64th's commanders, who were aware that the advance was likely to leave their right flank in the air.

The Knochgraben as seen from Herbebois. *H.P von Müller's Estate*

Continue uphill to the forest and **stop** at the T-junction with a wide dirt track (*Chemin de la Montagne*). In February 1916 there was a French infantry observation post here. The decorated obelisk standing nearby will be discussed later in this chapter.

The French observation posts in Herbebois provided clear views over German lines and approach routes. The cluster of buildings in the centre of the picture is Soumazannes. *Wim Degrande*

Defending Herbebois: 164th Infantry Regiment, 51st Division
The regiment responsible for the defence of Herbebois had the sort of intimate knowledge of the sector that came from months of occupation. The 164th Infantry, part of the Verdun garrison, had first arrived there in October 1914 at a time when the front was not settled and there were

50

The Military Governor of Verdun, General Coutenceau. *Author's collection*

The honour guard of the 164th Infantry Regiment. *Author's collection*

regular scraps and skirmishes back and forth. Over the months a trickle of deserters arrived, many of them ethnic Poles, while regular patrolling brought information about German movements, occasional prisoners and, on New Year's Day 1915, an event so unusual that everyday work stopped. At 2.45pm, the 164th's advanced posts near Soumazannes were startled by the arrival of a mounted German officer accompanied by an interpreter and a bugler. Conducted at his request to the subsector commander, Second Lieutenant Mommessin – a young man with one year's training at St. Cyr and who had been commissioned the moment the war broke out – the officer handed over an envelope addressed to the Governor of Verdun, General Coutenceau. Such an unusual event required immediate action and Mommessin, accompanied by a staff officer from 72nd Division, took the envelope to the general in person. To everyone's surprise, it turned out to contain a coloured lithograph of the Crown Prince of Germany with a handwritten message in German wishing his chivalrous adversary a happy New Year. With polite indifference General Coutenceau forwarded the envelope and its contents

Azannes

The view from the trench mortar position on the Cap de Bonne Espérance in 1916. Azannes is in the trees in the centre of the picture. *Landesarchiv Karlsruhe 456 F 106 Nr. 18, Bild 15*

to the man actually in charge of operations at Verdun, the Third Army commander General Sarrail, who sent it on to General Joffre.

This apparently quixotic act was the Crown Prince's way of acknowledging another unusual event that had taken place almost a month earlier. On 1 December 1914, with a new German regiment at the *Cap de Bonne Espérance*, the 164th launched a raid to find out who was there. Two men were killed on each side, the Germans panicked and fled, and the French retired, taking their dead comrades with them. However, before retiring two members of the patrol cut the ears off the German dead and brought them back, claiming that their captain had told them to do it; he claimed it had been a joke. The usual patrol reports were submitted without mentioning the barbarous act and it might have remained unknown had it not been for the Germans putting up notices along the front accusing the 164th of infamous behaviour. Revolted by the mutilation of the two Germans, and concerned about the consequences that it might have for the future, a young second lieutenant decided to take action alone. On 5 December he left his post in Herbebois and, with a white handkerchief for a flag, approached the German advanced line in order to express his profound regrets, and those of his company, for the mutilation. The officer to whom he was taken realized that this was too big a matter for him and the young lieutenant was first taken to Azannes for interrogation, and then blindfolded and driven to meet a senior officer who, although he did not know it, was the corps commander, General von Gündell. To him, the lieutenant explained that everyone had been sickened by the incident and also that the perpetrator had been executed, which was not true. Gündell, who was charmed by the initiative shown, accepted the explanation and offered tea and cake before sending the lieutenant back through the lines, once again blindfolded. However, by the time he got back the lieutenant had been reported for abandoning his post and communicating with the enemy contrary to orders, and he was locked up. Things looked very bad at first but, when the details of the affair reached General Sarrail, he decided that a transfer to another corps would be punishment enough. Nobody wanted the affair of the ears to become well known and it was not in the interests of the army for news of either the mutilation, or the lieutenant's escapade, to spread. Among French senior officers, opinions on the Crown Prince's gesture were divided over whether it was an affectation, a bad joke, or an elegant anachronism. For General von Gündell it was simply a farce.

The Crown Prince's action was not repeated twelve months later, by which time matters had become more serious. Throughout January 1916

Heavy guns moving up to Azannes. *Wim Degrande*

Preparing the access to a trench mortar position close to the road from Azannes to the Cap de Bonne Espérance. *Landesarchiv Karlsruhe 456 F 106 Nr. 19, Bild 12*

there was daily shelling of Herbebois; wagon convoys rumbled through the night, heavy goods were unloaded – it sounded like rails and stakes – mining and construction could be heard, and observers spotted new listening posts and newly cut gaps in the wire. The days passed with everyone on high alert and working frantically to improve the defences before the blow fell.

When dawn broke on 21 February Herbebois was defended by 2nd Battalion, 164th Infantry, supported by infantry and machine gunners from the 243rd Infantry and a detachment of naval gunners manning a long range 164mm naval gun. The use of naval guns on land had first been considered in 1913 in response to delays and difficulties in developing heavy artillery to counter long range German guns. Following tests on land, several 140mm naval guns were brought to Verdun in October 1914; they were followed in 1915 by three 240mm and two 164mm pieces, one of which was installed in Herbebois. The orders for the Herbebois gun, marked 'extremely urgent', involved first extending a light railway line by several kilometres to bring the gun into the area and then constructing the concrete emplacement. This was followed by the excavation of over seventy metres of underground galleries to provide accommodation for the gunners and storage for explosives and shells. Progress was slower than it might have been, partly because of the rocky nature of the ground, and partly because the noise and movement involved had to be masked from enemy observers, whose nearest positions were less than two kilometres away. The gun was finally in place on 7 August 1915; its target was a 380mm 'Long Max' naval gun then under construction in Bois de Warphemont, some sixteen kilometres to the northeast.

The flooded pit for the 380mm 'Long Max' naval gun in Bois de Warphemont. *Author's collection*

The battle begins
Finally, just when everyone had given up hope, the rain stopped. On 20 February the wind changed, the weather cleared, the Crown Prince issued his orders, and when the assault troops peered out of their dugouts the next day it was to see a swaying line of observation balloons and a sky full of German planes. The first round, a 380mm shell fired by the very piece in the Bois de Warphemont that the Herbebois gun was to target, gave the signal for scores of other guns to start to prepare the way for what the Corps artillery was calling the 'parade march' of the infantry to Verdun. For days before the start of the offensive German gunners had been telling any infantryman who would listen that the mighty array of guns assembled on the northern front would create a curtain of fire behind which the infantry could simply stroll into Verdun, collecting souvenirs as they went. Not everyone was convinced, especially those who had served on the Eastern Front and considered the artillery there to have been relatively ineffective. A few doubtful voices were raised but, as everyone was heartily sick of the war and just hoped that this would be the final offensive, most men allowed themselves to be persuaded. A member of 10 Company, Infantry Regiment 24, remembered the opening bombardment very clearly:

'At 9am [German time] the level of fire grew even greater. We were so nervous in the dugouts that we could hardly stand it. The only clear sound was crash after crash from the field howitzers and the huge 210mm howitzers that were smashing the enemy's first position. Everything else was just a sort of general thundering from the heavies and the superheavies ... that were shelling their batteries, forts and positions in the rear ... it sounded as if the four horsemen of the Apocalypse were riding out. Sometimes the noise was like an express train, then it was like a waterfall thundering over a cliff, screeching, booming... It was the most extraordinary noise you could imagine and as we could not hear it properly inside the dugout we kept going outside to listen... At 10am there was a gigantic roar and the dugout shook. Was that the enemy guns? No, it was just our trench mortars going into action and the noise they made drowned everything else. Now everyone had to go outside to see what was happening, and we stood there watching the shells fly into the air as if they weighed nothing – the biggest ones weighed well over fifty kilograms. They seemed to hang for a second before plunging straight down and a minute later there was a huge cloud of black smoke and an almighty explosion.'

A German heavy trench mortar in position. *Tom Gudmestad*

A German heavy trench mortar in position. *Tom Gudmestad*

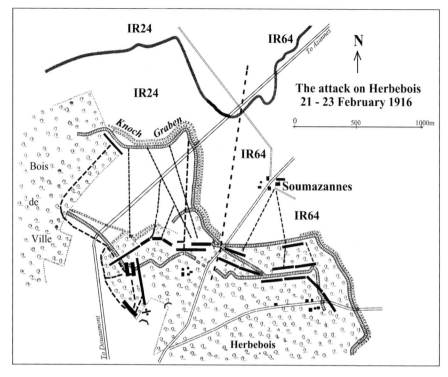

IR24

IR64

To Azannes

N

↑

IR24

The attack on Herbebois
21 - 23 February 1916

0   500   1000m

Knoch Graben

IR64

Bois

Soumazannes

de

IR64

Ville

To Douaumont

Herbebois

Impatient, tough, and used to success, the assault units waited through the hours of ear-splitting noise for the signal to move.

Infantry Regiment 24
It came at 4pm on 21 February. Bursting out of their lines and racing forward, Infantry Regiment 24 swiftly captured the Knochgraben. Now the artillery observers could come forward. Rockets were fired, signallers followed with reels of telephone cable, and the first group of prisoners came through, shocked men in horizon blue and steel helmets who had been captured in a dugout. But when the 24th tried to go on they immediately ran into heavy fire from positions in the wood that the hours of shelling had not destroyed. Pressing on – the orders were to advance without regard to casualties – they managed to reach the first line but were forced back by a vigorous French counter attack that pulled in every man available, including the cooks and quartermasters. By then darkness was falling and, with further progress impossible, the 24th took cover where they could. Casualties had been heavy; many of the assault commanders were already out of action and lines of men lay dead at the edge of the wood. All in all, it had not been a good day and an NCO

58

In the rear, a German band entertains the troops. *Author's collection*

cheerfully greeting new arrivals with the news that it was impossible to get forward and that everyone had been killed or wounded was roared at to shut up before his loose talk did any more damage. Everyone spent a freezing night in the open. At midnight it began to snow and in the morning the coffee was frozen.

Infantry Regiment 64
On the left, Infantry Regiment 64 had been more successful. Both assault regiments had received the same orders: seize the first line and hold it, then reconnoitre the second line to see whether further bombardment was needed. Climbing out of their start trench and heading through the prepared gaps in the wire, the leading wave – infantry supported by specially trained pioneers, heavily equipped with steel helmets, flamethrowers, machine guns, grenades and explosives – headed down to Soumazannes and took their first prisoners – men who had moved forward into No Man's Land to avoid the shelling. Leaving them to find their own way back to the German lines, the attackers were pressing on uphill towards their first objective when bursts of machine gun fire tore into them from the right. While their right stopped, their left swung hard left, hit the edge of the wood, got through the wire, and cleared part of the first line with flamethrowers and hand grenades. Almost ninety men were lost in the process, some of whom were blown up by their own insufficiently secured hand grenades as they clambered through the wire.

Two French trench mortars loaded: a heavy "crapouillot" and a small Cellerier mortar. *Tom Gudmestad*

The memorial to Infantry Regiment 64 stands in Azannes II German Cemetery. *Author's collection*

With their right flank still in the air, the 64th spread out in the wood. Later, reinforcements arrived and together they spent an uneasy night.

French and German accounts of the assault on Herbebois on 21 February differ markedly. While the Germans complain of determined resistance from largely undamaged defences, the French report a deluge of shells, crushed shelters, smashed guns and men buried alive. The bombardment quickly destroyed all but one of the telephone lines and messages had to be carried by relays of runners whenever the bombardment allowed. At 9am the naval gun had gone into action and immediately attracted heavy salvoes of shells from a 305mm Skoda howitzer, which did little damage. The sight of German troops massing at Soumazannes had brought a flurry of rockets, lamp signals and runners demanding urgent artillery support and, while it came too late to prevent the Germans from capturing part of the first line, the defenders were able to regroup and they were ready. When night fell Herbebois was still in French hands, as were the neighbouring centres of resistance of Ornes and Bois de Ville, so on the whole the day had not been too bad. During the night reinforcements were pushed up and a number of counter attacks were launched that were unsuccessful in retaking lost ground but brought in a number of prisoners and prevented any German advance.

22 February

The German plan for the next day involved another frontal attack at 12 noon to clear Herbebois and push on to the next line of hills. Infantry Regiment 24 was to move off first, with Infantry Regiment 64 following. It had been an icy night; no one had slept for more than a few minutes, and constant French shelling had caused heavy casualties among the front line troops and broken up communications with the rear. The gunners were still talking confidently about curtains of fire and souvenir collectors but both light and heavy artillery were missing their objectives – one firing too short and the other too long – and there were bitter comments about gunners and sharp questions about the lack of forward observers in the Knochgraben, the first objective of the previous day.

A German field artillery observation post. *Author's collection*

A French position in Herbebois. *Author's collection*

During the night a reconnaissance patrol had reported lines of strongly held French positions buried deep in underbrush and abatis behind banks of undamaged wire and as soon as the assault troops moved off it became clear that the morning's preparatory bombardment had again left the French defences largely intact. The 64th made some headway, capturing an observation post and taking a number of prisoners, but it was at the cost of another five officers and over 260 men. As for the 24th, they got nowhere at all. Urgent calls for artillery support only brought a promise of flamethrowers and eventually an observer from a field gun battery who, to the astonishment and fury of everyone in earshot, announced that he could not carry out observations in the wood anyway. The only good news was that on their right the 5th Infantry Division had finally managed to break through Bois de Ville. That provided the 24th with an opportunity: instead of attacking Herbebois frontally, they would use the newly conquered positions in Bois de Ville to attack it from the flank. Two infantry companies were immediately ordered forward; but darkness was falling and casualties were so high that the battalion commander ordered almost everyone back, leaving only a few sentries in place.

At the end of the second day's fighting the general opinion was that the whole thing was a complete cock up and that another frontal assault would be senseless. Everyone was frustrated. The 6th Division was used to succeeding in any task it was given but all the courage displayed had counted for nothing and they were losing trained and experienced men at all levels who would be difficult to replace. As they prepared for another freezing night without hot food or shelter, everyone agreed that it could not go on.

23 February
German orders for the third day involved a three hour artillery preparation followed by yet another frontal assault 'without regard to casualties', accompanied by a flanking attack from Bois de Ville. Everyone had been hoping for clear weather but it was cloudy, which meant no aerial observation, and there was a delay while new telephone lines were laid. The 64th was optimistic. A machine gun nest on their left flank had been spotted by a sharp-eyed observer and put out of action, and soon after zero hour another nest was captured and the whole line fought their way forward to the central ravine. However, on their right, the 24th was not so successful. Waiting in shallow scrapes on the slopes below Herbebois, where the leading units had been pulled back to avoid friendly fire, the men had their first hot food for thirty-six hours and watched as a couple of trench mortars were dug in. This time they were to be supported by pioneers and steel helmeted assault troops from Sturmabteilung Rohr;

German dead gathered up and awaiting burial. *Author's collection*

but after two terrible days expectations were not high, and when the frontal assault began it met the same problems as before. A junior commander in 1st Battalion described it:

> 'Orders received: advance at 12 noon without regard to losses. We hoped our artillery had been effective ... but we were bitterly disappointed. As soon as the first line moved off ... French bugles started to blow and we were hit by murderous rifle and machine-gun fire, much worse than the day before. Progress was unthinkable. Neighbouring units got nowhere. The enemy guns were shelling our positions with admirable accuracy. Our only hope was that the 5th Division had already reached Wavrille Hill and made the French positions in Herbebois untenable. It was futile to leave my first line close to the French unprotected and unable to advance, so I pulled the men back to their starting point to await events.'

Even flamethrowers could not clear the way forward: the streams of fire were not long enough to reach the French positions and the pioneers themselves became fiery targets. There was no hope of success and every man pinned his hopes on the flanking manoeuvre being carried out on the right. During the morning the 24th's last reserves had moved from the *Cap de Bonne Espérance* into Bois de Ville and slowly they made their way through a long communication trench into the tangled woodland at the western edge of Herbebois. Getting everyone into position took a long time, but by 5pm the 24th had two companies in the flank of the French defenders and two in the rear. The signal was given, and with everyone yelling and shouting, machine guns firing, drums banging and buglers blowing their lungs out they fell on the French line from the rear.

Lieutenant Johannes Wolff, who with his brother, Franz, was fatally wounded in Herbebois on 23 February 1916. *Author's collection*

Now the units pinned down in front of the wood could finally advance. 'We would not have been able to stand another day like this', wrote the commander of 10 Company, and continued

'At around 5.30pm, when the sun was beginning to set, we suddenly heard prolonged cheering in strong German voices coming from beyond the French second position. Then we knew: Herbebois was ours. I immediately ordered the rest of my company forward to the central ravine … The second position had been carefully laid out in tiers but it was only lightly held and there was no more resistance. However, thick masses of thorny undergrowth and wire made reaching the strongpoints and blockhouses very difficult and they were absolutely invisible from the front … I moved along the ravine. Our guns had been more effective here, and there was a gigantic jumble of smashed trees and torn up bushes that I could not get through.'

The naval gun

It was a patrol from Infantry Regiment 64 which found the naval gun. Being in a fixed position known to German observers, it had come under fire from the first day of the offensive. The observation posts, which were also well known, were soon smashed and, with telephone lines ripped up and no contact with the rear or with other batteries, the naval commander, Enseigne de Vaisseau Pieri, just had to do the best he could on the basis of prior orders. The ammunition was expended by the end of the first day and the ferocious bombardment meant there was no possibility of re-supply, so the gun crew retired to a nearby trench, where they were later joined by the naval observers from Soumazannes. The gun had not suffered much from the bombardment but it was clear that Herbebois

The 164mm naval gun in Herbebois. *H.P von Müller's Estate*

could not hold out indefinitely and on 22 February Pieri decided to destroy it, but the safety fuse failed and he remained in the wood. However, when the German flanking manoeuvre was successful the following day Pieri tried again. Once more the fuse failed, and with the Germans setting up a machine gun in plain sight, Pieri and a picked group of men approached the gun carefully, unscrewed the breach and carried it away before laying into it with pickaxes.

Unteroffizier Paul Riedel, 9 Company, Infantry Regiment 64, died in Herbebois on 22 February 1916 and was buried where he fell. An admired officer, his memorial reads 'He died for us. Our love is his reward.' When his body was exhumed in 1999 two other men were found to have been buried with him. He lies today in the German cemetery in Labry. *Jan Carel Broek Roelofs*

By the time the Germans attacked from the rear the French knew that Herbebois was outflanked and they had started to withdraw. Abandoning everything they could not carry they headed south as fast as they could, leaving the Germans to enjoy the hot food already prepared in the field kitchens. Gradually the Germans rounded up the stragglers and by midnight Herbebois was finally in their hands: but the cost had been terrible. Eleven hundred men of the 6th Division had fallen in the three day battle, with some battalion and company losses approaching 50%. It was no better for the defenders. Of the two battalions of the 164th Infantry defending Bois de Ville and Herbebois, only six officers and 377 men answered the roll call, while the 243rd had lost over 400. In Ornes the 164th's remaining battalion held out for a further twenty four hours until, faced with the risk of encirclement, most of the remaining defenders slipped back to Bezonvaux, a couple of kilometres to the south.

Two former German cemeteries
Infantry Regiment 24 **(5)**
The fine obelisk standing close to the track originally formed the centrepiece of a small enclosure, some sections of which remain on the ground. Information in three languages is available on the panel. The

cemetery stands close to the regimental boundary between the sectors attacked by Infantry Regiment 64, to your left, and Infantry Regiment 24, to your right. Note the only remaining upright memorial, which commemorates *Offizierstellverträter Otto Drähn*, 5 Company, who died in a hand grenade battle in Caillette wood in May 1916 (see Walk No 4). At least two other victims of the appalling fighting in Caillette wood were originally buried here: *Leutnant der Reserve Bernhard Stollbrock*, 5 Company, and *Vizefeldwebel Otto Schneidereit*, 8 Company, who were killed on 22 and 24 May respectively. During the 1920s all the bodies were exhumed and reinterred in the German military cemetery in Ville-devant-Chaumont, a little over two kilometres from Azannes.

This memorial stood in the centre of the cemetery laid out by Infantry Regiment 24. *Author's collection*

Most of the men were buried in a mass grave; but two have individual plots: *Otto Drähn* lies in grave 3–327, while *Leutnant Jürgen Freiherr von Eynatten*, a platoon commander in 8 Company who died in the Fort Douaumont sector on 27 May 1916, lies in grave 3–334. After the exhumation much of

Lieutnant Freiherr von Eynatten. *Author's collection*

the stone from the cemetery was removed and used to build the grotto and shrine at Azannes that you saw earlier. It included some handsome decorated plaques which were, alas, stolen a few years ago.

The cemetery in its heyday. The decorated plaques stolen from the grotto in Azannes were those seen here on the gateposts. *Wim Degrande*

Two days after capturing Herbebois, elements of Infantry Regiment 24 went on play a leading part in the capture of Fort Douaumont, the most important fort in the whole Verdun system. For the story of how they did it and what happened afterwards see my book *Verdun – Fort Douaumont*.

3. Rheinisches Pionier-Bataillon Nr.30 (6)

The damaged memorial to this battalion stands by the side of the track on a low bank roughly 130 metres to the left of the obelisk. It is difficult to see in summer because the bank is completely overgrown but if you approach it from the top if the bank you will find it. The memorial has suffered from frost damage and there is no plan to restore it. The readable names all belonged to 4 Company.

By February 1916 this highly experienced battalion's war service had included the Marne, Champagne, the Argonne Forest, and a period in the Verdun sector between October 1914 and May 1915. The first days of the Verdun offensive saw them supporting the actions of XVIII Corps by cutting wire, removing obstacles, bridging trenches and shell craters, and repairing and building roads and tracks. They were always heavily laden with wire cutters, scaling ladders, hand grenades, flame throwers, and various forms of improvised explosive devices for dealing with wire or concrete obstacles. Before action their tasks included reconnoitring the expected break-through points and ensuring the prior destruction of wire and flanking positions; once the position was captured they constructed shell proof dugouts, organized drainage and camouflage, and dug communication trenches between the rear and the new front lines. In the central area of the battlefield, especially during the summer of 1916, they worked under particularly dangerous conditions, which often involved heavy labour at night and during shelling, often wearing gas masks. This battalion was particularly involved in the capture of Vaux village in March 1916, the capture and defence of Fort Vaux, and the defence of Fort Douaumont. *Gefreiter Franz Maréchal*, one of those whose barely legible names are recorded here, was killed at Fort Douaumont on 28 May 1916; while two others, *Unteroffizier Ernst Besecke*, and *Gefreiter der Reserve Johannes Kehlenbach*, died at Vaux village at the end of the ghastly month of March 1916. The German war graves list does not mention these men so perhaps their bodies were never found. Two other men named here died early in 1915, long before this cemetery was established: *Kriegsfreiwilliger Paul Weilenmann* and *Kriegsfreiwilliger Wilhelm Wirtz* died on 12 February 1915 at Flabas, a village to the north of Colonel Driant's positions in Bois des Caures, and their bodies must have been brought here during 1916. Wilhelm Wirtz lies today in block

The damaged memorial to 3. Rheinisches Pionier-Bataillon Nr.30. *Author's collection*

5 grave 54 in the German military cemetery at Damvillers; but Paul Weilenmann's name does not appear on the war graves list. During the 1920s all the bodies were exhumed and transferred to other cemeteries in the area.

From June - December 1916 Herbebois was sufficiently far behind the lines for camps and medical facilities to be established here and one of the camps was used by 4 Company until the French offensive of

A German working party take a break from building an observation post.
Tom Gudmestad

December 1916 brought the front too close for comfort and forced them to withdraw to a new site. In the first months of 1917 they returned to Herbebois to construct command posts and a defensive position called the *Herbeboisriegel* on the western side of the wood. The three observation posts you will see later on this tour may be a part of that. As retaliation for the French use of German prisoners of war in positions close to the front line, some 250 French prisoners of war were employed in building the *Herbeboisriegel*, and they also excavated some of the dugouts in *La Coupure*, the ravine running through the centre of Herbebois that you will visit later.

A comfortable German camp on a steep hillside. *Tom Gudmestad*

Herbebois in 1917 – 1918

From March 1916 to August 1917 Herbebois was a quiet and even enjoyable sector if the history of Leib-Grenadier Regiment 109 is to be believed. A camp on a wooded slope at the northern edge of Herbebois offered small huts and wooden barracks protected from artillery fire and a sheltered meadow in which men could sunbathe, enjoy sports, pick flowers, eat strawberries, and relax in fresh air and sunshine. It must have seemed like a real health resort but it all came to an end on 12 August 1917, when French preparatory fire for the counter offensive of 26 August began to smash into the wood. Although the counter offensive was stopped, Herbebois was once again in the fighting zone. One of the fortified lines constructed at that period, the *Hagen-Stellung*, ran through Herbebois and formed the main German line of resistance in the sector. Like the *Brabanter-Stellung* on Wavrille Hill, it comprised machine- gun posts, strongpoints backed by wire, and deep mined dugouts linked by galleries and tunnels. When Wavrille Hill fell to the French on 9 October 1918 the defenders, Infantry Regiment 137, withdrew to the *Hagen-Stellung*, where they managed to hold off small parties of French troops but were not strong enough to launch a counter attack. The next few weeks were uneventful and there was so little activity that the Germans began work on improving their positions. On clear days planes flew, there was a certain amount of shelling and occasional limited actions, but

A German regimental command post in Herbebois. *Wim Degrande*

otherwise Herbebois remained quiet until the Armistice, when coloured rockets on both sides of the line signalled the end of the war.

The walk continues
Return to the obelisk, then continue straight ahead along the track for just over one kilometre. At a T-junction with a wide grassy track, turn left and **stop (7)**. Face ahead. Before the German assault, an extensive cleared area on your left, known as *La Coupe aux Abris*, was the site of reserve shelters, dugouts and the command post of 2nd Battalion, 164th Infantry. There was also a small French cemetery here and there are substantial French and German workings close by. Not far inside the trees on the opposite side of the track and roughly in line are three German observation posts in various states of dilapidation which, when constructed, offered extensive views southwards **(8)**. They may be part of the *Herbeboisriegel* mentioned above. With the observation posts on

72

Two German observation posts. *Author's collection*

your right, continue ahead for roughly 500 metres and turn right downhill between blocks 113 and 112 **(9)**. Just before you reach the steepest part of the track note the substantial trench on the right which has numerous dugout entrances. These are German workings. The ravine ahead is the *Ravin des Renards*, which the 164th Infantry Regiment knew as *La Coupure*, and it is lined with dugouts. When you reach the bottom of the ravine, cross over to the other side, then turn left and walk for approximately 200 metres until you see some concrete remains on the right hand side of the track **(10)** and, on the left, a short section of railway line which has grown through a tree. Both appear to be the only remaining relics of the naval gun emplacement, which stood in this area. In winter it is clear that this part of the ravine was very heavily shelled and it remains very muddy.

Concrete remains on the site of the 164mm naval gun. Look for the short length of railway line in the tree opposite. *Author's collection*

A dugout, still with two beds, close to the gun position. *Author's collection*

Return to Azannes

Now turn back and walk up the ravine, keeping the dugouts on your left. From 23 February 1916 to the Armistice Herbebois was in German hands and the front was to the south, which is to the left. That means that the dugouts in the hillside on the left were German, while any that you see on the right of the ravine were French ones from before February 1916. Continue ahead for approximately 1200 metres and **stop** at the T-junction with the Chemin St. André **(11)**. The Germans called this long straight track the *Kegelbahn* (bowling alley) and it led directly from the *Cap de Bonne Espérance* through French lines towards Fort Douaumont. Saint André Farm, a substantial group of buildings standing at this junction,

A well established German camp, possibly in this ravine. *Wim Degrande*

became an important German strongpoint but was destroyed during the war and has never been rebuilt. The French prisoners of war who were forced to build the *Herbeboisriegel* were camped there. Now turn right and follow the Chemin St. André for two and a half kilometres. At the crossroads by St. Donat's cross, **stop (12)**. This is the *Cap de Bonne Espérance* and the site of the German position raided by the 164th Infantry's notorious patrol on 1 December 1914. Continue straight ahead downhill and after one kilometre take the right fork to return to Azannes

GPS Waypoints Tour No. 2

1. N49°17.464' E005°28.031'
2. N49°17.543' E005°27.789'
3. N49°17.182' E005°27.120'
4. N49°16.765' E005°27.016'
5. N49°16.482' E005°26.622'
6. N49°16.492' E005°26.738'
7. N49°16.117' E005°26.324'
8. N49°16.089' E005°26.322'
9. N49°16.168' E005°26.576'
10. N49°16.078' E005°26.913'
11. N49°16.932' E005°26.598'
12. N49°17.015' E005°26.817'

Tour No. 3

March–October 1916

Damloup Battery, La Laufée, Chenois and Fumin Sectors

Distance: Approximately 8 kilometres
Duration: A half day's tour, without a visit to Fort Vaux. Adding a visit to the fort could make it a full day's tour
Maps: IGN 3112ET or IGN Blue Series 3112 Ouest.

A circular tour of the Chenois, La Laufée and Fumin Sectors of the Right Bank, beginning and ending at Damloup.

Memorials on this tour: Corporal Emile Mettra, Private Henri Laurent, Privates Henry and Robert Poulet, Chasseur Jacques David, Corporal Gilles Moné, Aspirant Maurice Coutier, Corporal Louis Boutard and fourteen men of the 106th Infantry Regiment.

There is a steep uphill stretch of roughly 750 metres to the site of Damloup Battery but the rest of the tour is reasonably level or downhill. There are no cafés or toilets anywhere on the tour and you are only likely to meet other visitors if you visit Fort Vaux, so make sure you are carrying everything you need.

Warning: When walking this sector, visitors should stay on the paths and keep away from the edges of holes. Do not attempt to enter any concrete structures or climb on the roof of La Laufée.

The tour begins at the cemetery on the rue de la Laufée, Damloup **(1)**, a village on the D24, roughly twelve kilometres northeast of Verdun. Park by the cemetery and follow the sandy track towards the wooded Meuse Heights. The Heights are cut by deep ravines that not only provide access from the plain but also divide them into a series of promontories that French military engineers used before the First World War to site forts, fieldworks, batteries and other positions. At the crossroads in the tracks at the end of the football field, **stop**. Fort Vaux stands on the promontory

76

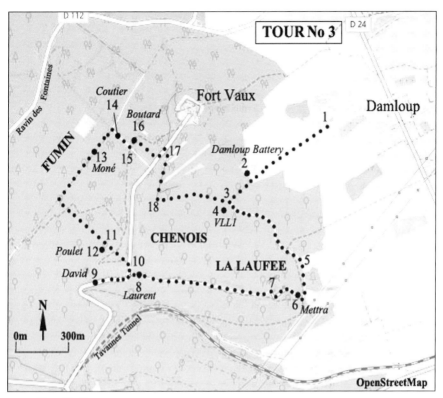

Tour No 3.

to your right front, Damloup Battery was straight ahead; the La Laufée fieldwork is to your left front with another battery beyond it and a host of smaller positions in between. It was to a farm near Damloup that the garrison of Fort Vaux was brought by the Germans after the fort surrendered on 7 June 1916.

Damloup
Between August 1914 and February 1916 Damloup was several kilometres behind the front line and it played little part in events. However, it became important once the offensive began, because it controlled access to the ravines ahead and, in particular, to Fort Vaux. The French had always regarded the Damloup sector as a quiet one and for the Germans, who overlooked the village from the far hillside to your right, it seemed scarcely defended at all. Surrounding most of it was a trench running some fifty metres in front of the houses, which was not well organized because the proximity of the German lines meant work could only be carried out at night. In addition, the secondary defences

Damloup in January 1916. *Wim Degrande*

were few, in a poor state of repair, and the wire was broken. For most of the time the trench was only lightly held, with a few sentries outside and everyone else sheltering in the cellars. That included the machine gunners, who waited inside for a call from the sentries before going into action.

It was 1 June before the Germans got close enough to Fort Vaux to attack it directly and the following day troops from Grenadier Regiment 3 and Infantry Regiment 105 swooped on Damloup to prevent it being used as a base for counter attacks on the fort. They took the garrison (1st Battalion, 142nd Infantry, which had only just arrived) completely by surprise and reached the houses before there was any response. While some of the attackers pushed on, only stopping when they ran into their own artillery fire, others combed through the cellars, capturing machine guns and taking over 500 prisoners. Captain Boyer, 3rd Company, described what happened:

'After being shelled all night we suddenly heard machine gun fire: There was a shout of 'To Arms!' … we scarcely had time to grab a rifle before a horde of Germans was on us… Waves of men kept coming and the company just melted away. I was alone with a runner in a bit of a trench waiting for a counter attack but the Germans saw us. They surrounded us, waving hand grenades in the air. We were out of ammunition and resistance was impossible.'

Better than capturing the men was finding the cellars stocked with plentiful rations, tinned meat, chocolate, brandy, and much else.

The first the French knew about it was when an out of breath sergeant burst red faced into the regimental command post a kilometre or so behind the French front line, shouting that the Germans had got Damloup. It was scarcely believable; the last message from the garrison had reported 'Sector quiet. Little shelling as long as we do not show ourselves' and now it was in German hands. To make matters worse, as more information filtered through, it became clear that although machine gunners on the Meuse Heights had seen the German assault and fired on the attacking waves, they had been too far away to stop them and Damloup had fallen without a fight. An immediate counter attack was ordered and a company rushed forward, but the attempt failed with heavy losses and the survivors withdrew. It took a long time for the French artillery to realize that Damloup had changed hands and until well into the afternoon French guns were still shelling the old German lines. They made up for their mistake later; but by then the Germans were bringing up supplies and digging in.

French prisoners captured at Damloup. *Wim Degrande*

For the next few months, despite coming under continuous artillery fire that smashed the houses and drove everyone underground, Damloup was a logistical and medical centre of the first importance for the Germans. Nothing moved there during the day; but at night the ruined village came alive as carrying parties and ammunition columns moved up, rations and

79

The ruins of Damloup. *Wim Degrande*

hot food arrived, the wounded were evacuated, and relieving units hastened forward. Even in the dark it was a feared place and no one lingered. The village remained in German hands until the counter offensive of 24 October 1916 brought French troops to the edge of the Meuse Heights once more and forced the Germans to abandon it. After the war, some of Damloup's territory was designated Red Zone and the owners were expropriated. With the ground completely churned up, the ruins unrecognisable and boundaries lost, the remainder had to be re-surveyed before the preliminaries to rebuilding – clearing the ground, burying the dead, filling shell holes and ponds with debris from the village and laying tracks – could begin. In the end it was decided that the level of destruction was too great for Damloup to be rebuilt on the old site and a new village was developed around the crossroads with the D24.

Now walk ahead; follow the track as it enters the forest and rises steeply. After approximately 600 metres, turn right **(2)** into an open field, face the plain and **stop**. There is no doubt about the spectacular views and clear fields of fire offered by this line of hills, which at the time were largely unforested. Unless first shelled into submission, French positions on the Meuse Heights were almost impregnable.

Damloup Battery
In addition to forts and fieldworks, the steps taken by the French to fortify this area between 1874 and 1914 included batteries and firing positions known as *retranchments* (entrenchments). These were long concrete or

The destroyed entrenchment would have been similar to this almost undamaged one not far from the Ouvrage de Froideterre. *Author's collection*

stone parapets divided by buttresses into recesses in which troops could take shelter during shelling. This bare hilltop was the site of both. The entrenchment, which was one of a whole series of similar positions along the edge of the Meuse Heights, stood at the far end of the field commanding the plain, while the important Damloup Battery, constructed in 1881 for six light calibre guns but armed in 1914 with four 90cm pieces, stood to the rear of the field behind a steep earth rampart. Today there is little trace of the battery and the entrenchment has completely disappeared. Fort Vaux stands less than one kilometre away on the next promontory to your left.

Aerial view of the Damloup Battery-Fort Vaux sector. *Author's collection*

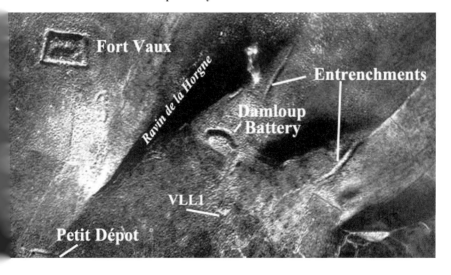

Once Fort Vaux had fallen on 7 June the Germans could devote their energies to Damloup Battery. An assault planned for 4 June was postponed because the flamethrowers failed to arrive in time and the grenadiers were suffering from friendly fire. Infantry Regiment 99 took over, more attempts were planned, but French resistance was so strong that it was 23 June before German troops got anywhere near the battery; when they did they were pinned down by such storms of machine gun fire that it was nightfall before the survivors could withdraw. Two days later a heavy howitzer bombardment forced the French to withdraw. However, by the time the Germans reached the battery the defenders were back and once again the attack got nowhere. With normal tactics failing, the Germans came up with a new plan. In the early hours of 3 July a rain of trench mortar shells forced the defenders, a unit of the 172nd Infantry, to keep their heads down. The storm troops moved forward, German guns

Shelling destroyed Damloup Battery so completely that the only thing to be seen is the rampart that fronted the guns and this last trace of an arched shelter. *Author's collection*

A similar arched shelter for a battery close to Fort Belleville. *Author's collection*

laid a barrage across the area and once the storm troops were in position other mortars began firing duds. While the French were sheltering from the expected explosions, the Germans rushed forward, hurling grenades into shelters and depots; ammunition exploded, men were burned, panic set in and the survivors quickly surrendered. A simultaneous attempt to capture a nearby infantry shelter was a failure; but at last the Germans had the battery and they immediately set about organising it. Over the next few days the French made nine attempts to retake it, finally managing to reoccupy part of it on 7 July but losing it entirely on 11 July during an all-out German assault on the whole sector launched after a twenty-six hour bombardment. Damloup Battery was only recaptured on 24 October 1916.

Now return to the main path, turn right uphill and **stop** at the T-junction in the tracks. Face directly ahead **(3)**.

La Laufée, Chenois and Fumin

The regimental and family memorials on this tour commemorate French soldiers who fell between March and October 1916, with most of the deaths occurring in June. From March to June 1916 the German effort on the Right Bank of the River Meuse concentrated on pushing towards the strategic heights secured by the Froideterre fieldwork, Fort Souville and Fort Tavannes. This involved a preliminary action to capture Fort Vaux, which in the end took three months, and during that time progress was disappointing. By the beginning of June, with casualty levels rising and little to show for it, the German High Command needed a decisive success and on 23 June 1916 ordered a major assault on the Right Bank with the aim of bursting through the centre of the French line and reaching the last line of hills before Verdun. The attempt was unsuccessful and, after a final effort on 11 July, the Fifth Army was ordered on the defensive. However, that did not mean that the battle came to an end; for the rest of the summer there was intense fighting in this area as the Germans concentrated on retaining the gains already made, straightening their line and capturing limited objectives that would allow them to hold on.

The French front in this part of the Right Bank was divided into three sectors – La Laufée, Chenois and Fumin. In June 1916 all three were violently attacked by the German 50th Infantry Division and were defended by the French 12th Infantry Division, whose four regiments – from right to left the 106th, 132nd, 54th and 67th – held a front line without organized trenches under a continuous torrent of shells and bursts of machine gun fire. Crouching in shell craters, isolated from one another

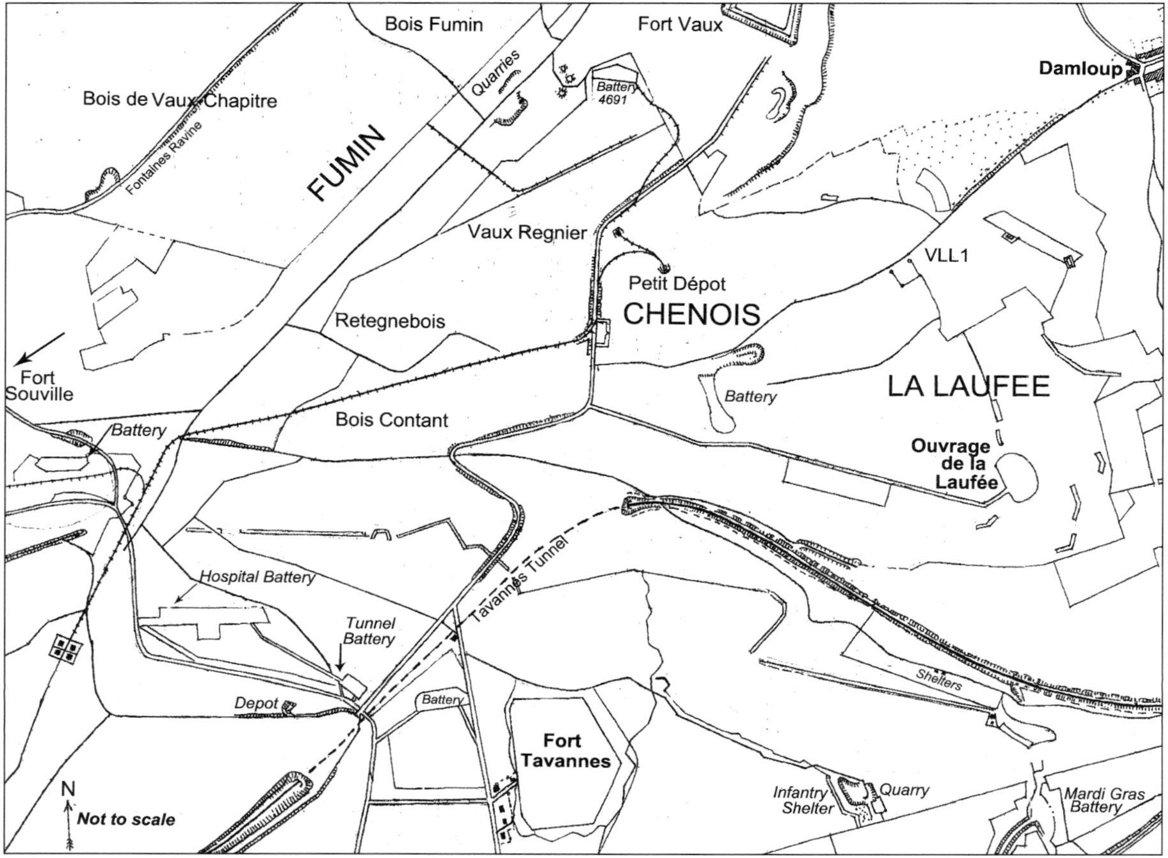

The La Laufée, Chenois and Fumin Sectors.

Damloup

VLL1

LA LAUFEE

Ouvrage de la Laufée

Battery

Shelters

Mardi Gras Battery

Infantry Shelter

Quarry

Fort Vaux

Petit Dépot

CHENOIS

Battery 4691

Vaux Regnier

Quarries

Bois Fumin

FUMIN

Retegnebois

Bois Contant

Tavannes Tunnel

Fort Tavannes

Battery

Tunnel Battery

Depot

Bois de Vaux Chapitre

Fontaines Ravine

Hospital Battery

Battery

Fort Souville

N

Not to scale

84

and often unaware of other units, commanders and men on both sides lost touch, liaison broke down and communication was impossible. Casualties reached appalling levels, the wounded could not be evacuated, and the dead lay where they fell. Generally overlooked, and with the exception of Fort Vaux not well visited, the sectors you will walk today were as important to the eventual outcome of the battle as any of the main sites.

La Laufée Sector
Infantry Shelter VLL1 (Vaux-La Laufée 1)
Hidden by the trees on the other side of the track is a very ruined infantry shelter, so overgrown now that even in winter it is difficult to spot **(4)**. If you wish to see it, follow the beaten footpath that starts opposite the tree bearing block number 510. This shelter, often wrongly described in photographs as Damloup Battery, was built between 1899-1900 to provide accommodation for infantry serving in the sector.

Visé Paris n° ⸢48 ℕ 548 ⸗ *LES RUINES DE LA GRANDE GUERRE. — Env. de Verdun.*
Batterie de Damloup — **LL.**

This popular postcard view describes Infantry Shelter VLL1 as Damloup Battery. *Author's collection*

Designed to house a company, it offered seating for 200 in four rooms that were protected by a roof of reinforced concrete and walls two metres thick. There was a small kitchen and an outside latrine, while a heavy stone blast wall in front of the shelter protected the entrances. Under the decree of August 1915 that downgraded Verdun's status from an

85

independent fortress to a fortified region, strongpoints such as this were to be blown up if the enemy approached; however, once the battle began the need for protection from constant bombardment made it too useful to be destroyed and throughout the summer of 1916 VLLI served both sides as a command centre, first aid post and general shelter. It also became, as did any strong concrete construction, an ammunition dump – with frightful results.

From 17-27 June 1916 VLL1 was defended by the 106th Infantry Regiment. As a strongpoint close to Damloup Battery, it was a particular target for the German 210mm and 305mm howitzers and on 19 June part of the shelter collapsed on top of the machine gun section, burying men and guns alike. There was no chance of evacuating anyone quickly. German guns on top of Fort Vaux prevented any movement during the day and the wounded had to be evacuated at night, which was also the only time when supplies, rations and orders could arrive. The raging bombardment continued until the early hours of 23 June when the Germans launched an assault, but somehow the defenders managed to pull themselves together and the attackers were driven back. Two days later, after a period of reasonable calm during which many of the previous day's wounded were brought in to await evacuation, an avalanche of shells hit the shelter, setting fire to the signal rockets, blowing up a grenade dump and bringing down part of the roof on the men sheltering inside. The Germans finally captured VLL1 on 3 July 1916, lost it in hand to hand fighting nine days later, then recaptured it and held it until the French counter offensive of 24 October 1916. Throughout that period VLL1 was only a couple of hundred metres behind the front line and the constant French bombardment blew away the blast wall, exposed the entrances and destroyed three of the rooms.

The current state of VLL1 makes it impossible to imagine what it looked like before it was destroyed. This is Infantry Shelter MF2, an identical construction near the Ouvrage de Froideterre. *Author's collection*

The memorial plaques on the side of VLL1. The bigger plaque reads 'From *Les Revenants du 106 RI* in memory of their comrades of 1 Machine Gun Company buried by a shell on 21 June 1916: Dardet, Desclandes, Enoq Godard, Hazé, Herouard, Lequenne, Letonqueze, Lina, Melin, Moreau, Thimotée, Vachez'. *Author's collection*

When withdrawn on 27 June the 106th had lost over 900 officers and men, fourteen of whom were blown up or buried under rubble in this shelter. After the war, former members of the regiment, describing themselves as *Les Revenants du 106ième*, placed a plaque here to commemorate the thirteen machine gunners who died in the roof collapse of 19 June 1916. The years have taken their toll and today the names are worn and difficult to read. Beside it a smaller plaque commemorates Corporal René Guerraux, 1 Company, who died in the explosion and fire of 25 June – proof, if any were needed, that in that nightmare battlefield of chaos and death any shelter from the shells, however damaged, was better than none.

Plaque in memory of Corporal René Guerraux, 1 Company, 106th Infantry Regiment, who died in the shelter on 25 June 1916. It was placed there by his parents. *Author's collection*

87

A small French observation post. *Author's collection*

If you have visited the shelter, return to the main track and walk ahead, keeping the edge of the Meuse Heights on your left. After 700 metres the views open out and you will see a small French observation post on the left by a track that runs steeply down to the plain **(5)**. As the post is undamaged, it may have been built after the counter offensive of 24 October 1916. A short distance further on a bench offers a good view and a place for a picnic. Continue until you reach the memorial to Corporal Emile Mettra, 3rd Battalion, 44th Infantry.

Corporal Emile Mettra, 44th Infantry **(6)**
The 44th Infantry had the distinction of being the first French regiment to lose a man in the war, and that was even before it had been formally declared. On 2 August 1914, with general mobilization less than twenty four hours old, Corporal Jules Peugeot was commanding an advanced post outside the village of Jonchery, southeast of Belfort, when a German mounted patrol was spotted. The sentry who raised the alarm was cut down and in the mêlée that followed Peugeot was fatally wounded and the German patrol commander was killed. Each was their country's first casualty.

For the 44th that sudden encounter with reality was only the start of bloody service at the Marne, on the Aisne and in Champagne. The beginning of the Verdun offensive found them at the foot of the Meuse Heights. The weather was icy, the bombardment intense, and the casualty lists lengthened day by day as the Germans pushed forward. Soon most of the French second position was in German hands but a few places still held out, including Bezonvaux, a village on the plain some five kilometres north of where you are standing. Bezonvaux, which was held by 3rd Battalion, 44th Infantry (Mettra's battalion), was important to both sides because it controlled two ravines that provided access from the Woëvre Plain to the French second and third positions. On 25 February 1916 the Germans launched a fearsome bombardment on Bezonvaux and the surrounding area, isolating it and preventing the arrival of reinforcements. As the defences were smashed, new ones were thrown up only to be smashed in their turn, and little by little the village was surrounded. The battalion commander was wounded, the senior company commander, a sixty-six year old volunteer, was also wounded and, with the position hopeless, his replacement finally ordered a withdrawal. By then the one remaining line of retreat was covered by a German machine gun and only about thirty men managed to escape. Among those captured in Bezonvaux was an American, Frank Musgrave, a graduate of Tulane University in New Orleans who had previously practised law in Texas. Musgrave, who had volunteered for the French Foreign Legion as soon as war broke out, had served with other American volunteers in the vicious Champagne fighting of 1915 before being transferred to the French infantry. Between 21 and 29 February the 44th suffered over 1100 casualties and the War Diary describes the three companies defending Bezonvaux as *à peu près anéanties* – almost wiped out. And now they were back.

The 44th returned to Verdun on 13 April and moved up to the front the following day. At this stage of the battle the French front line on the Woëvre Plain formed a salient in which there were a number of defensive bastions. These included Damloup and Dicourt Farm, a cluster of buildings standing some 800 metres to the south of the village. It was here that the 2nd and 3rd Battalions took position, with the 2nd in Damloup and the 3rd, including Mettra's 10 Company, between the

Bezonvaux during the battle. *Tom Gudmestad*

village and the farm. The distance between the French and German front lines varied from 500 metres to two kilometres and the sector was not well organised. Fire and communication trenches were either unfinished or non-existent, while continuous enemy shelling disrupted the arrival of supplies, prevented communication and movement, and constantly hampered attempts to improve the position. While the 2nd Battalion in Damloup could shelter in the cellars of the old houses, the 3rd Battalion had to make shift as best they could. Conditions were beyond awful; torrential rain filled the trenches with mud and water, 'hot' food arrived cold between 11pm and 1am from field kitchens 800 metres away and without any means of reheating it, and the men carried four days' rations in case no food got through at all.

A mud spattered ration party by a field kitchen. *Author's collection*

The battalions' main tasks were to strengthen the position and to patrol their front to check on work being carried out by the Germans; occasionally prisoners were taken and once a deserter arrived. Despite the shelling and the awful weather, they managed to complete some communication trenches and even to extend the wire; but there were casualties every day and on 22 April these were particularly high, with twenty three men killed or wounded and nineteen missing. The latter included thirty two year old *Emile Mettra*, a native of Nuits St. George, in the Côte d'Or region of France. His body was later found and buried here, then exhumed after the war and reburied in plot 9748 in front of the

Emile Mettra's original grave. *Author's collection*

Ossuary. His death certificate, originally dated 23 April 1916, was later amended to 23 August 1916, at which time the 44th was on the Somme. Could 23 August be the date on which his body was found? We shall probably never know. Corporal Mettra is also commemorated on a plaque in the Tavannes section of the Ossuary.

La Laufée fieldwork **(7)**
Now continue ahead and **stop** at the junction with the track leading to the courtyard of La Laufée. This fieldwork was built for two purposes: to control the railway between Verdun and the pre-war German border and to cover the gap between Fort Vaux and Fort Tavannes. Originally

just a small infantry post built in the late 1880s, La Laufée was modernized in the first decade of the twentieth century by the addition of a concrete barrack block, a rotating 75mm gun turret, observation posts and water cisterns. A plan to surround the fieldwork with a ditch with armed bunkers linked to the barracks by shell proof underground tunnels was abandoned in August 1914 and instead it was surrounded by wire. When Verdun's status was changed in August 1915 the garrison was withdrawn and it was only replaced in May 1916, by which time La Laufée had suffered months of shelling and been used as a command post, stores dump and shelter by anyone in the sector. As a result, the new garrison had to spend time restoring order, carrying out repairs and clearing rubbish before they could hope to defend it properly. With so many unauthorized troops inside the barracks there was barely room for the garrison, and it took intervention at the highest level to restore order and force non-garrison troops to leave. With Fort Vaux under constant bombardment a little more than 1300 metres away, the garrison was placed on the highest alert and ordered not to evacuate or surrender the fieldwork even if surrounded.

From the start of the offensive La Laufée was targeted by every calibre of shell and it quickly became unrecognizable. The earth ramparts were flattened, the wire was torn up, the outside magazines and stores were completely smashed, and one of the observation posts on the roof was blown out of its bed. However, the roof remained intact and the barracks were habitable. The 75mm turret defended both Fort Vaux and Damloup Battery, and during the siege of the fort it proved such a thorn

The courtyard of La Laufée during the battle. *Author's collection*

The 75mm turret survived the Battle of Verdun only to be removed during the Second World War, leaving this gaping hole on top of the barracks. *Author's collection*

in the German side that it was violently shelled for days. As the rotating turret was too important to the general defence of the area to risk its destruction, the commander was ordered to restrict firing to cases of dire emergency and thus for the next few months La Laufée mainly functioned as an observatory. The German summer offensives of 1916 brought their front line to within 350 metres of La Laufée; with the remaining observation posts providing devastatingly clear views of German movements, there were increased, but unsuccessful, attempts to destroy both them and the turret. An inspection report drawn up after the battle found that the barracks, the remaining observation post, and the 75mm turret had survived the tons of steel flung at it; while there were scratches and dents on the turret's heavy steel cupola and some slight damage to the rotation mechanism, that had not prevented it from firing almost 2000 shells. After repairs were carried out, the turret was able to support the French counter offensives of 24 October and 15 December 1916. After the war it was estimated that La Laufée had been the target of at least 40,000 shells of all calibres at a cost to Germany of eight to ten million francs – all to destroy a fieldwork that had cost less than one million francs to build and equip.

In 1917 various improvements were made with the aim of strengthening the fieldwork and protecting it from a surprise attack. A machine gun bunker was added to cover the open courtyard, an electricity generator was brought up, a well was dug and a tunnel system excavated under the barracks to provide shelter for the garrison, storage space and remote access. It remained in the hands of the French army and during the construction of the Maginot Line the rotating turret and underground tunnels were repaired and reinforced. Stripped of metal, including the gun turret, during the Second World War, possibly by German engineers, it was later abandoned by the French army and gradually forgotten.

Leaving La Laufée behind you, continue along the track for approximately one kilometre and **stop** at the field memorial standing under trees on the left just before you reach the road. Face the memorial. Tavannes railway tunnel is in the cutting to your left.

Chenois Sector
Private Henri Laurent, 171st Infantry **(8)**
If they were to be successful on 23 June 1916 the Germans had to capture a number of French positions which were certain to be strongly defended. In the Chenois Sector the most important of these were Tavannes and Souville, two forts standing a couple of kilometres from the German front line. Preparation for the offensive started early on 21 June with a colossal bombardment. Colonel Bagès, commander of 24 Brigade, described the result:

'All the communications are destroyed, the runners can't get through; they can't even get from the brigade command post to division. There's thick dust over the whole sector and an avalanche of shells everywhere (green cross [gas]) giving off a horrible stink. We can't see anything and can't hear anything either.'

It was followed by an assault across the entire sector that drove a deep salient into the French lines. On the French right, where a battalion of the 54th Infantry held a line of shell craters, two companies were wiped out, two others were captured, and a huge gap appeared in the line. Lieutenant Delacourt, 54th Infantry:

'In 1st Battalion…3 Company was almost completely destroyed along with two sections of 4 Company. That made a gap in the line and the Germans got through and took 1 and 2 Companies from the rear. It was all over very quickly; the machine guns were out of action and only a few rifles still worked but the men who were not wounded – about two hundred of them – defended themselves as well as they could with hand grenades. They were soon overcome and the survivors were rounded up.'

The attackers flooded through the gap and surrounded a battalion of the 132nd Infantry, which spent the next five days fighting for its life. They also captured an underground powder magazine known as the *Petit Dépot*, which for months had formed a shell proof command post just behind the French front line, and by the time they stopped they were less than one kilometre from another vital piece of French defence: the 1200 metre long Tavannes railway tunnel. The commander immediately

Tavannes tunnel in 1916. *Tom Gudmestad.*

ordered it to be evacuated, organised for defence and urgently called for reinforcements. Two battalions of the 171st Infantry were alerted and at 9pm on 23 June they moved off to rendezvous with their guides; but after a long day of ferocious fighting no one was there. With every minute critical, infantry and machine gunners set off along the only available communication trench, picking up guides from other units as they did so. Eventually one of the attacking battalions arrived at a command post not far from where you are standing only to find that no one knew the whereabouts of the troops they were to relieve, nor even if any had survived. Conditions were chaotic in the extreme, with the ground a sea of craters, under a continuous bombardment of the utmost violence and with little in the way of organized positions. The second battalion was delayed for hours and the commander already in position requested that that the attack be postponed, but his request was rejected. Finally, at 7am on 24 June everyone was in place; the two battalions were deployed on either side of the road a short distance ahead of where you are standing (D913a) and ordered to advance cautiously until they met either the 54th or the Germans. If any of the 54th were found they were to remain in place as the 171st moved forward.

It was a disaster. Moving off in broad daylight at 10.30am the 171st ran into a wall of fire and in less than an hour they had lost several machine guns and fifty percent of their effectives, including a battalion commander and sixteen other officers. With further progress impossible they were ordered to dig in and hold every inch of ground. During the night some units were relieved, the lines were sorted out, liaison was established to left and right, and even some remnants of the 54th found, although they had no idea where they were. When dawn broke on 25 June the 171st's lines formed a pincer around the German positions, with the base of the pincer close to the *Petit Dépôt*. Wishing to straighten the lines, the divisional commander ordered the 171st to launch a surprise grenade attack on the depot without artillery preparation. At 8pm grenadiers and infantry assembled in a trench in this area and were led forward. They made two attempts to reach their objective, one launched at midnight and the second a couple of hours; later but each time they were repulsed with heavy casualties and after four days in the line the 171st was withdrawn with the loss of two thirds of its effectives. They had, in the words of their Regimental History, 'sacrificed themselves with their usual devotion to re-establish the situation and resist the German Army's most furious attacks... The chaotic hillocks of Chenois and La Laufée witnessed acts of heroism which history may one day remember.'

French troops in the cutting leading to the entrance to the Petit Dépot.
Author's collection

No one knows what acts of heroism may have been performed by twenty six year old *Private Henri Laurent*, who died on 25 June 1916 somewhere in this area. His name is not mentioned in the regimental War Diary, which only lists officers. Born in Baudoncourt, Haute Saône department, on 29 January 1892, his name appears on the war memorial there but it is not in the French war graves list, so either his body was never found or it was returned to his family. The situation in this sector in late June 1916 being as chaotic and violent as it was, it is more likely that he, and the two unnamed companions remembered here, simply disappeared.

The recently refurbished memorial to Henri Laurent.

The older, simpler version, which does not mention his two companions.
Author's collection

Now continue to the road (D913a), turn left and walk ahead. At the sign reading *Les Jumeaux* [The Twins], turn right into the forest and walk up to the cross commemorating *Jacques David* **(9)**. Although signposted here, the twins' memorial is actually some distance away and will be visited later in the tour. Chronologically, however, their story fits in here.

Private Henry Poulet and Private Robert Poulet, 333rd Infantry
The chaotic hillocks of Chenois and La Laufée may not have been particularly high but they nevertheless provided those that held them with views over those that did not, and they also blocked the route to Fort Souville. After failing to reach the fort on 23 June, the Germans tried again on 12 July and then again 1 August when, after swamping the sector for several days with gas and high explosive, things went better. Disoriented and stunned by days of shelling and reduced in some parts of the front to a handful of men in a horrible unrecognisable wasteland, the French were unable to resist. A gap appeared between the units on either side of the D913a, and the Germans burst through.

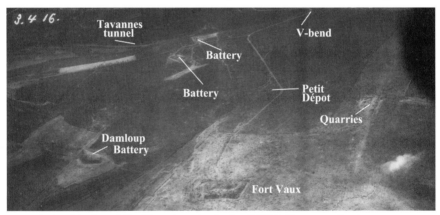

An aerial view of the Chenois sector in April 1916. *Harry van Baal*

They pushed the French line several hundred metres back, reached the V-bend of the road not far from where you are standing, overran two batteries and finally came to a halt two hundred metres from Tavannes Tunnel and less than a kilometre from Fort Souville. Once again the tunnel was put on alert. An immediate counter attack recaptured the batteries and closed the gap in the line; but it had been a close shave and over the next few weeks the French attacked repeatedly to regain the lost ground. Although they succeeded in forcing the Germans several hundred metres back, it was at the cost of daily heavy casualties and the lines remained fragmentary and precarious.

Part of one of the batteries overrun on 1 August 1916. *Author's collection*

This area was wooded at the start of the Battle of Verdun but by the beginning of September months of fighting had turned it into a wasteland of splintered tree stumps, trenches that were little more than scrapes, and corpses, some of which, adding horror upon horror, remained inexplicably upright. It was into this awful wasteland of dirt, noise and fear that the 333rd Infantry, a reserve regiment from eastern France, moved during the night of 8–9 September 1916. Their ranks included *Privates Henry (also known as Jean) and Robert Poulet*, twins born on 9 February 1895 at St. Honoré les Bains in the Nievre department. At 5am on 9 September, following a ferocious German barrage all along the line, infantry and machine gunners moved into position.

The Poulet twins. *Author's collection*

99

The 333rd's War Diary describes 9 September as a 'quiet day', with intermittent bombardment but no infantry activity. There was some heavy calibre shelling on the first and second lines and a trench mortar bombardment of the *Petit Dépot* but nothing else. That did not make it any less tragic for the Poulet brothers. The War Diary report, which gives no details, mentions 140 casualties, including Robert and Henry Poulet, who were both hit by the same shell. Each brother generously urged stretcher bearers to evacuate the other one first but Robert was too badly injured to be moved and he died shortly afterwards. Henry, who was not fully aware of the gravity of Robert's injuries, was evacuated to a hospital outside Verdun, where he died nine days later. He was buried as Jean Poulet and lies today in Landrecourt Military Cemetery in plot 116. Robert's name does not appear on the French war graves list, so we may assume that his remains were lost.

Henry Poulet's grave in the French cemetery at Landrecourt. He was buried as Jean. *Author's collection*

Commanding officers wrote warmly to the boys' parents about their cheerful natures, the deep bond between them, their courage, discipline and devotion to duty. One can only hope that it brought some comfort. They are commemorated in the small private memorial that stands in the forest several hundred metres from here on the site of a provisional battlefield cemetery, now cleared. Their names also appear on the war memorial at St. Honoré les Bains and on a plaque in the *Petit Dépot* section of the Ossuary.

Chasseur Jacques David, 50th Chasseurs à pied
With both sides at Verdun trying to gain control of strategically important positions on the Right Bank before bad weather brought fighting to an end, it was the third week of September before relative calm descended. When it did, it masked the beginning of preparations for a major French counter offensive on the Right Bank that was aimed, first, at recapturing Forts Douaumont and Vaux and, second, at pushing the German lines far enough back to free the city from the danger of a surprise attack. The counter offensive was commanded by General Mangin and the date chosen was 24 October; and in preparation

General Mangin, who commanded the French counter offensive of 24 October 1916. *Author's collection*

for it the assault troops trained intensively in tactics involving mixed units of machine gunners, pioneers and lightly armed, fast moving infantry. When the day came there were three infantry divisions in the front line, with the 38th on the left, the 133rd in the centre, and in this sector the 74th Division, commanded by General de Lardemelle. Supporting them were three more infantry divisions and over 650 guns of all calibres, including two mighty 400mm howitzers whose targets were Fort Douaumont and Fort Vaux. The orders were for the first wave to move off at 11.40am, reach the first objective and pause before beginning the second movement at 13.40pm. The task of the 50th Chasseurs was to reconnoitre and if possible occupy Fort Vaux after the second objective had been reached and consolidated.

After four days of roaring artillery preparation the first wave moved off behind a rolling barrage. In this sector progress was good on the left and right, and many prisoners were taken in their dugouts as the troops moved forward. However, in the centre of the sector the attackers, who included the Chasseurs, failed to get through No Man's Land before the German counter barrage began, and they ran into a strongly held front line, unbroken wire, and violent machine-gun fire from, among other strongpoints, two quarries and the *Petit Dépot*. During the summer German pioneers had improved ventilation in the depot, created new exits, and enlarged it with a series of underground rooms; but it remained overcrowded, hot, frightening, difficult to access, and subject to continuous bombardment. It had acquired a terrible name: *Stützpunkt Hölle* [Strongpoint Hell] but was too important to give up without a fight.

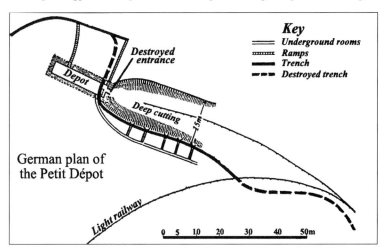

German plan of the Petit Dépot.

At 1.40pm the troops on the left and right of the sector moved off again and soon reached the second objective, leaving the Chasseurs stuck in the centre. Desperate not to be held up any longer, their commander gave the order to advance regardless of the machine guns, and two hours later the 50th reached the second objective but went no further. It was 10pm before the *Petit Dépôt* was cleared and the rest of the centre could move forward. During the night everyone worked hard to organize the new position; but a violent bombardment undid much of the work and caused more casualties. Among the ninety eight officers and men of the 50th Chasseurs who became casualties that day was twenty nine year old *Jacques David*. The War Diary says nothing about the circumstances of his death but the Chasseurs had a first aid post in a small quarry at the side of the D913a, a short distance from where you are standing, and it is possible that he died there. He was buried on this hillside in a provisional cemetery but his body was later exhumed and reburied in front of the Ossuary in plot 443.

Jacques David's original gravestone, with handwritten inscription. *Author's collection*

General Mangin was infuriated by General de Lardemelle's failure to reach Fort Vaux and replaced him. French troops finally re-entered the fort in the early hours of 2 November 1916 after the Germans had withdrawn. For further information, see my book *Fort Vaux*.

From here return to the D913a, turn left and walk ahead. Just after the bend turn left into the forest between block 509 and 510 **(10)**. After roughly 200 metres, turn left **(11)** on to a rough forest ride to visit the *Poulet Memorial*. (*Note: If you are not using a GPS, the turn into the ride has a dilapidated hunter's hide accessed by a long ladder on the left and a beech tree with three trunks on the right.*) After roughly a hundred metres you will reach a cleared area **(12)**. The Poulet Memorial, which is only small, is on the right but hidden by a tree as you approach the clearing. Long forgotten, this sad little memorial has recently become a feature of many battlefield tours.

The woodland memorial to Henry and Robert Poulet. *Author's collection*

From the Poulet memorial, return to the main track, then turn left and walk ahead. The track crosses the highest point in the Chenois Sector and the scene of desperate fighting throughout the summer of 1916. While forestry clearance and replanting means there is little to be seen on the right, shell craters and trenches are everywhere on the left. Continue to the T-junction with the wide *Chemin de la Vau Régnier* and then turn right. You are now in the Fumin Sector. Before the Battle of Verdun this track ran through a wide corridor of open ground that allowed for clear observation between Fort Souville to your left rear and Fort Vaux to your right front.

Fumin Sector
Corporal Gilles Moné, 67th Infantry **(13)**
After 350 metres an opening on the right just before yellow gas line marker 274 brings you to a modern cross standing close to the track. It commemorates twenty two year old *Gilles Moné* and his companions of the 67th Infantry who fell in this sector on 22 June 1916 after a day of unparalleled violence. In the early hours of 20 June, the 1st and 2nd Battalions, 67th Infantry, took up position here facing Fort Vaux, which was less than one kilometre away. A bombardment of indescribable fury raged across the sector from early morning on 20 June until late afternoon the following day, when the exhausted and stunned 67th was attacked by strong waves of infantry. Scraping up reserves of strength that they scarcely knew they had, *Gilles Moné* and his companions managed to hold them off; but on their right the Germans broke through, demolishing a battalion of the 54th Infantry in the process. The regimental commander immediately ordered a counter attack. Corporal Pierre Pasquier took part:

Fort Vaux from the Chenois sector with no place to hide. *Author's collection*

French troops in one of the quarries in the Fumin sector. *Author's collection*

'We attacked like madmen; the major was with us. We didn't even hear the bullets whistling past. We charged with bayonets, took back one of the 54th's trenches and forced the Germans back into a quarry where we dealt with them. A few men from the 54th escaped and managed to join us. The Germans tried again before nightfall but they were repulsed with heavy casualties. My company was down to forty men.'

With their right flank in the air, the 67th spent the night patrolling their front and trying unsuccessfully to re-establish liaison. At 8am the next day the divisional commander ordered them back but the regimental commander refused, saying that his men would not understand why they should abandon ground they had held successfully the previous day and there was no clear line to withdraw to. The general agreed, and the 67th took up a new position in quarries on the other side of the *Chemin de la Vau Régnier*, facing the gap in the line. There they remained, suffering all day from the appalling bombardment, half asphyxiated by gas, blinded by dust, hungry and thirsty. The artillery duel was frightful. Sapper André Charroy, 9th Génie, wondered how he had survived:

'Our guns were getting louder, so were theirs; where would it end? The German bombardment was unimaginable. Air, ground, everything was shaking… everything was blowing up in a fury of iron and fire… I don't know how we survived those thirty six hours. We ate our rations, we drank what we had, we smoked, but there was no taste, no pleasure. We just did everything mechanically, like automata. All around us explosions were shaking our little scrapes, drowning us in noise.'

At 4am on 23 June the Germans launched their main assault. They were relying on phosgene gas to silence the batteries in the centre of the French line on the Right Bank and it was there that they had the greatest success. However, the effects of the gas soon wore off and by the afternoon French guns were firing again, exhaustion had set in, and the German advance had stalled. However, there was no let up for the 67th, and by the end of the day their only reserves were a single infantry platoon and one machine gun section. The War Diary

The memorial to Gilles Moné.
Author's collection

comments that if those dreadful days were one of the most painful periods of the regiment's history they were also one of the most glorious; but between 19-24 June over one thousand men became casualties. As the War Diary only mentions officers by name, *Corporal Moné* must be one of the thirty nine unnamed men listed as killed on 22 June. His body was never found and he was posthumously awarded the Croix de Guerre and Médaille Militaire.

Aspirant Maurice Coutier, 60th Field Artillery **(14)**
Now return to the *Chemin de la Vau Régnier*, turn right and walk ahead. The long quarry on the left is one of those defended so desperately by the 67th Infantry between 22-24 June. After roughly 200 metres, turn right on to the *Sentier de Vaux* between blocks 509 and 508 and **stop** at the memorial to *Maurice Coutier*, which is on the left. Face back the way you have come. Fort Vaux is roughly 600 metres to your right rear.

Coutier, a probationary officer with the 60th Field Artillery Regiment, was killed here on 2 March 1916 while serving at a forward observation post. The gunners had arrived at Verdun on 24 February and were immediately ordered up to Fort Souville, where at first light the following day the colonel reconnoitred the area and ordered the batteries into position. There were no trees on this hilltop at the time and the view from here, which stretched for several kilometres, included the Fort

A French field artillery battery on the move. *Author's collection*

Douaumont plateau and the deep valley between Fort Douaumont and Fort Vaux. After the Germans captured Fort Douaumont on 25 February they turned their attention to Fort Vaux and that meant gaining control of the valley. Their first attempt to do so was launched on 2 March and was supported by a bombardment with gas and high explosive that forced the field gunners to wear gas masks all day. 'Not an inch of ground was spared the fury of the shells', according to the 60th's War Diary, which reports guns blown up and overturned, ten horses dead and twenty three gunners killed or wounded. They included the battery commander and twenty two year old *Maurice Coutier*, who had volunteered for the post of observer in this exposed position in place of men with family responsibilities. This was reflected in his posthumous citation in Army Orders, which referred to him as having the highest sense of duty and was always volunteering for the most dangerous missions. Coutier's name does not appear in the French war graves list, so either his body was returned to his family or it was never found. He died one month before his 23rd birthday.

Maurice Coutier's memorial. *Author's collection*

The forward observation post stood close to Battery 4691, a permanent position constructed before the First World War as part of the general fortification of the Verdun Sector. It was completely destroyed during the battle and today only a few scattered blocks of concrete and the outline of low earthworks remain to show where it stood. It was recaptured on 24 October 1916.

Corporal Louis Boutard, 132nd Infantry
With the Coutier memorial behind you on the left, walk ahead for one hundred metres and turn left into the forest by a wooden post bearing a small sign reading *Fôret d'exception* **(15)**. Walk straight ahead for 150 metres, crossing the former site of the battery just mentioned, and continue until you reach the memorial to twenty three year old *Corporal Louis Boutard*, 9 Company, 132nd Infantry **(16)**, who died somewhere in this area on 21 June 1916 whilst resisting the same German assault as Gilles Moné. He was one of fourteen named officers and 144 unnamed men to die that day and his body was never found.

Thanks to recent forest clearance, visitors may now pay their respects to Corporal Louis Boutard without hunting through deep undergrowth. *Author's collection*

Until a few years ago this memorial was in deep forest and it is a tribute to the efforts of a very small number of interested local people that these paths have been created and the site cleared.

The 132nd had two battalions defending this sector on 21 June, with one being relieved by a battalion of the 54th Infantry just as the assault began. The Germans broke through the line, destroyed the relieving battalion, flooded through the gap, and surrounded the 132nd's remaining battalion, the 3rd. What happened next was described by Captain Chazot, 9 Company, who was Private Boutard's commanding officer:

'Dawn on 21 June, a deluge of shells and trench mortars, an avalanche of rifle grenades. We immediately lost a lot of men. A section of 12 Company, neighbour to my Third Section, was completely wiped out by the trench mortars. The bombardment got worse and at around 5 pm it reached such a level of violence that I thought an attack must be coming... I immediately sent the runners to warn my four section commanders to make sure every man was at his post. I was right, because the runners had scarcely completed their mission than the German guns raised the range

Two dejected French prisoners in Damloup. *Wim Degrande*

and the assault began. At the same time a terrific barrage fell on Chenois Wood. The company was ready for them and, despite serious losses and being attacked from all sides, we held off repeated attacks and inflicted terrible damage. The Germans were not discouraged and kept on attacking but they got nowhere.

I was just preparing my report when one of my sergeants … ran up. He commanded the only automatic rifle team in the battalion and, still out of breath, he explained that he had smashed his rifle and escaped …but that 10 and 11 Companies had been taken prisoner along with a battalion of the 54th, and that the Germans were trying to outflank us. The battalion commander was completely unaware of the situation and I immediately sent the sergeant to warn him.'

It was not only the battalion commander who did not know what was happening. No one at brigade or divisional headquarters knew either. Captain Chazot again:

'After the storm of the assault came a period of terrible anxiety for the valiant men of 9 Company. As division staff assumed that our battalion had been taken prisoner, our position was subjected to an intense bombardment by our own guns. The 75s literally poured shells on us, and it required great efforts from all our officers and NCOs to keep the men steady. To hold out against the enemy is nothing, but to feel one's life is threatened by his own side defeats the courage of even the strongest man.

Sergeant Magnier and a corporal volunteered to try and re-establish liaison with the regimental and brigade commanders. [The sector] was infested with enemy patrols but they managed to get through and brought back [the brigade commander's] congratulations and the order to hold on whatever the cost...

Over the next few days there were several attempts to relieve us but they all failed. We could see for ourselves that our troops could not possibly get through that barrage of shrapnel. It was absolutely impenetrable.

We had nothing left to eat. We suffered terribly from thirst, because it was very hot and we only had water from a little spring and it kept getting blocked up. The water was muddy and smelt of corpses...We had many wounded and the first aid post soon became too small. We were living in a morgue; no sooner had we buried someone than shelling brought the body up again.'

After the fighting, the awards. French troops receiving decorations at Verdun. *Taylor Library*

Fort Vaux today. *Author's collection*

They finally limped back to Tavannes Tunnel on 27 June – a journey of less than two kilometres that took them three hours. Ten days in the sector had cost the 132nd almost 1300 men.

With the Boutard Memorial behind you, follow the path to the D913a. Cross the road and walk towards Fort Vaux for approximately fifty metres, stopping when you reach a forest track which joins the road on the right between blocks 521 and 515 **(17)**. A visit to the fort may be convenient at this point. A full description of the siege of the fort, together with detailed tours of the interior and exterior, are to be found in my book *Fort Vaux*. Return here after visiting the fort.

Return to Damloup
To return to your car, take the forest track here, pass the barrier and walk ahead for approximately 300 metres. At the bottom of the dip where two tracks join on the left, **stop (18)**. The infamous *Petit Dépot* stood a couple of hundred metres to the right of where you are standing; but shelling has filled up the deep cutting that led to the entrance and there is nothing to be seen of it today. From here, turn left along the second track between blocks 520 and 516. This is the *Chemin de la Laufée*. Continue for approximately 750 metres **(3)**, then turn left downhill between blocks 517 and 516 to return to Damloup.

GPS Waypoints Tour No. 3

1. N49°11.968' E005°29.157'
2. N49°11.757' E005°28.623'
3. N49°11.672' E005°28.483'
4. N49°11.654' E005°28.476'
5. N49°11.460' E005°28.934'
6. N49°11.310' E005°28.941'
7. N49°11.335' E005°28.752'
8. N49°11.392' E005°27.831'
9. N49°11.367' E005°27.538'
10. N49°11.438' E005°27.800'
11. N49°11.519' E005°27.683'
12. N49°11.489' E005°27.626'
13. N49°11.852' E005°27.583'
14. N49°11.913' E005°27.756'
15. N49°11.877' E005°27.828'
16. N49°11.933' E005°27.914'
17. N49°11.884' E005°28.068'
18. N49°11.713' E005°28.003'

Tour No. 4

March–October 1916

St Michel Ridge, Ravin de la Poudrière, Ravin de Bazil, Caillette Sector, Fleury, The Louse

Distance: Approximately 17 kilometres
Duration: A whole day's tour
Maps: IGN 3112ET or IGN Blue Series 3112 Ouest.

A circular tour of the central sectors of the battlefield on the Right Bank, starting at the Fort Souville picnic site.

Memorials on this tour: Second Lieutenant Robert Flornoy, Privates Jacques Salamite and Henri Ruèche, Corporal André Rachel and companions, Chaplain Alexandre Constant, Sapper-Miner Emile Bretonnière, Sapper René Roiné, Second Lieutenant Jacques Legros, Second Lieutenant Maurice Dubuc, Private Saint-Just Borical, Second Lieutenant Jacques Lyon, Private Paul Sommières, Second Lieutenants Henri Herduin and Pierre Millant.

This tour involves a number of steep stretches and a walking stick may be useful. Toilets and a café are available during opening hours at the *Abri des Pèlerins* café/restaurant, behind the Ossuary, and at Fleury Memorial museum; access to the toilets at the Memorial is free but you need a museum ticket to access the café. There is a roofed picnic kiosk with seating close to Fleury Memorial car park and benches and tables where this tour begins. There will be visitors around Fleury and Abri 320 but otherwise you will meet no one for long stretches of this tour, so make sure that you are carrying everything you need.

Warning: When walking this sector visitors should stay on the paths and keep away from the edges of holes. Do not attempt to enter Fort St. Michel, the Poudrière, old dugouts or any concrete structures.

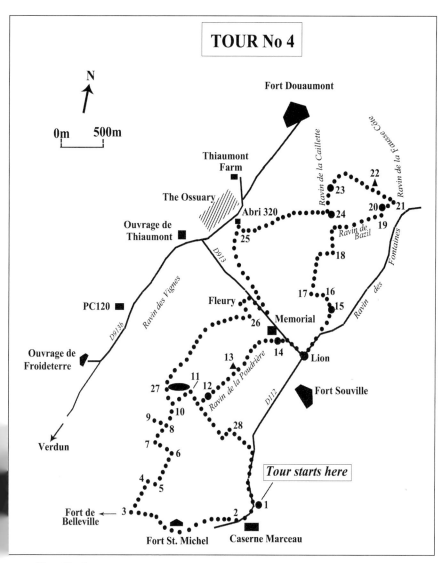

TOUR No 4

N

0m   500m

Fort Douaumont

Thiaumont Farm

The Ossuary

Abri 320

Ouvrage de Thiaumont

Ravin de la Caillette

Ravin de la Fausse Côte

22

23

20 21

24

19

Ravin de Bazil

25

18

PC120

Fleury

Ravin des Vignes

17 16

15

Ravin des Fontaines

26

Memorial

D913b

D913

Ouvrage de Froideterre

13

14

Lion

27

11

12

Ravin de la Poudrière

D112

Fort Souville

10

9

8

28

7

6

Verdun

4

5

Tour starts here

3

1

2

Fort de Belleville

Fort St. Michel

Caserne Marceau

Tour No 4.

The tour commemorates French soldiers who died between March and October 1916. It begins at the picnic site on the D112 close to Fort Souville, where there is plenty of parking **(1)**. Leave your car and return to the D112, then walk in the direction of Verdun until you reach the battered water tower (signposted *Réservoir d'eau*) that stands among

113

The entrance to Fort Souville after the battle. The drawbridge has been destroyed and rubble fills the ditch. *Author's collection*

trees on the left. This is one of two similar towers that served the Caserne Marceau, an important barracks, now ruined, which stood nearby. Close to the tower was a specially constructed shelter that served as a collecting

Caserne Marceau before 1914. The administrative services of the army at Verdun were based here. *Author's collection*

Caserne Marceau is in ruins today. The building in the picture is the second building on the right in the pre-1914 view. *Author's collection*

point for wounded needing transport by motor ambulance to Verdun. Generally speaking, such shelters comprised long, corrugated iron roofed shells that were dug into hillsides or banks and reached by a short flight of steps. Once inside, the wounded were triaged, given basic treatment, and waited on piles of straw for the ambulances to arrive. They often had to wait for hours. Many of the ambulances were driven by young American volunteers, who made the dangerous journey up the D112 from Verdun without lights and frequently during bombardment. One such volunteer, John H McFadden Jr of Philadelphia, vividly described the journey from their headquarters south of Verdun along that very road to an aid post close to Fort St. Michel and only a short distance from here.

'Going to the *poste de secours* from [headquarters], you pass through Verdun, and continue on a wide, level road for about one kilometre, and then you start up a very steep hill which continues for five kilometres right to the *poste de secours*. This road is very narrow and sufficiently dangerous from a driving point of view apart from the fact that it is shelled continuously day and night.

A French aid post in the Verdun sector. *Author's collection*

Indeed, one of the duties of [the Section Director] is to go up every morning at daybreak with a couple of men and fill up the holes which have been made during the hours of darkness so that our cars will not fall into them...

The day driving is comparatively nothing. The part, however, for which [drivers] deserve all the praise you can give them is their work at night. Naturally no lights are allowed, and I have never seen a country that can produce darker nights than that district. Therefore let one try and imagine the difficulties of starting from the top of that hill with a car full of wounded and driving down a narrow hillside road in a blackness impenetrable for more than a yard. In fact, if it were not for the light given by the firing of the guns and hand-grenades the work would be well-nigh impossible; and what makes it more difficult still is that all the traffic starts at night when the ammunition is brought up to the various batteries and you are continually finding teams of horses almost on top of the car before you have any idea of their presence. The round trip from the *poste de secours* to the hospital takes from two hours and a half to three hours, which averages a speed of about ten kilometres an hour...

No matter how carefully a man drives at night, a number of accidents are bound to occur. In one night there were six ...the White *camion* one night went into a ditch; two cars went head on

An American ambulance on a good road waiting for repair. *Author's collection*

into each other in the darkness; two more cars went into ditches and another fell into a shell hole.'

At the water tower, cross the road and enter the forest on a hard dirt road. This is block 577 (**2**). Continue ahead for about 800 metres and stop when you reach a yellow and black painted barrier on the right and a sign reading *Terrain Militaire. Défense d'Entrer.* Fort St. Michel stands in the trees on the right.

Before and during the First World War this road served a whole series of defensive works of the inner fortress line, including batteries, concrete or stone retrenchments, ammunition depots and two forts: Fort St. Michel here and Fort Belleville a little over two kilometres ahead. Built between 1875 and 1877 on sites where visible Prussian batteries had been established during the sieges of 1792 and 1870, these two forts protected communications into Verdun by river, railway and road, and flanked the fortifications on either side. In 1914 Fort St. Michel had four 90cm guns and two mortars on the rampart, with revolver guns and light artillery in the caponiers, but it was progressively disarmed as the war went on, particularly after the decision of August 1915 to downgrade the status of the Verdun *place forte* from a fortress to a fortified region. By March 1916 it had become clear that fixed fortifications still served a purpose and the forts on this ridge were regarrisoned and rearmed with machine

The damaged entrance and ditch of Fort St. Michel after the battle. Facing it on the horizon on the right of the picture is Fort Belrupt, which would have had any Germans who reached Fort St. Michel in its sights. *Author's collection*

guns. Fort St. Michel was frequently shelled, particularly during the German offensives of 23 June and 11 July 1916, when it formed one of the German objectives. After the battle, engineers excavated a system of deep rooms and tunnels under the fort to provide shelter during shelling and remote access. In 1918 a Pamard Casemate, housing two machine guns for close defence, was also constructed nearby.

Second Lieutenant Robert Victor Flornoy, 121st Heavy Artillery Regiment
In 1916 there were no trees on this ridge and, with clear views stretching over both sides of the River Meuse, it was a vital position for artillery and observers. On 8 March 1916 two batteries of the 121st Heavy Artillery took position not far from here and set up their command post in one of the magazines in Fort Belleville. The batteries were shelled and there were casualties, including the orientation officer, a twenty nine year old volunteer named *Robert Flornoy*. On 13 March Flornoy, whose responsibilities included reconnoitring possible battery positions, positioning observers and sending out patrols, had been making his way

to the battery commander's observation post at Fort Belleville when he was hit by a shell splinter and died shortly afterwards in the ambulance transporting him to the nearby military hospital. He was awarded a posthumous Croix de Guerre and after the war his family commissioned a memorial window in the church of St. Jean Baptiste, Avenue de la 43ième Division, Verdun. If you go to look at the window, notice the black doves that represent the three children he left behind. Flornoy lies today in plot 25 in the Faubourg Pavé Military Cemetery, close to the central cross. For the GPS waypoints for St. Jean Baptiste and the cemetery, see the end of this tour.

The commemorative window in the church of St. Jean Baptiste. *Author's collection*

Continue ahead for approximately 500 metres and turn right downhill between blocks 573 and 572 **(3)**. You are now following a route used by thousands of men in 1916 as they made their way towards the front or headed back to Verdun. This area was forested in 1916 and the trees sheltered communication trenches, first aid posts, supply dumps, dug outs, command posts and batteries, all of which attracted shelling and made it dangerous. At the T-junction **(4)** roughly 500 metres further on, turn right on the *Chemin le Tacot*. This is the old embankment for the *Petit Meusien* light railway, which before the war wound up from Verdun and across the Right Bank on its way to the Belgian border. You will meet it again later in the tour. After approximately 250 metres, turn left downhill between blocks 569 and 570 **(5)** and continue to a wide dirt road called the *Chemin du Clou* **(6)**. Turn left along the track, which after a short distance bends sharply to the left. Just before the bend you will see a short track running straight ahead. This cuts off a loop of the Chemin du Clou and you can take it or, if it looks very muddy, follow the loop. Once back on the main track, continue ahead for a very short distance and turn right on a grassy track running gently uphill **(7)**. Ignore any paths branching off to the right but continue ahead as the track becomes steeper and after about 150 metres turn left into the forest along a grassy ride at **(8)**. As you walk ahead look for two low white posts beside a flat memorial stone. (*Note: There is no signpost for this memorial, so if you are not using a GPS look to your left as you walk uphill and when you see a large pile of somewhat overgrown whitish rubble, return downhill to the nearest ride and turn right into the forest.*)

One of the military hospitals at Verdun. *Author's collection*

Privates Jacques Salamite and Henri Ruèche, 3rd Battalion, 119th Infantry **(9)**
One of the regiments moving up at the end of May 1916 was the 119th Infantry, a regiment which had previously served at Verdun and knew the battlefield only too well. During a much needed period out of the line for rest and reorganisation they had received reinforcements and been quartered on barges to the south of Verdun. Here the battle was out of sight but not out of hearing, and the noise of huge shells exploding only a few kilometres to the north was terrifying, especially to the new men, ten of whom were from the then French colony of Guyane. On 30 May 1916, the 1st and 3rd Battalions headed up the long communication trench from Verdun to St. Michel Ridge and down into these woods. No green and pleasant forest then; to Major Quenedey, the newly promoted commander of the 1st Battalion, it was a horrific place.

'The path we were following was a sort of whitish track cratered by shells and bordered by broken tree trunks and leafless bushes. Here and there a black shape, a dead horse with its legs spread out and swollen flanks, lying with its neck flat on the ground. From time to time a patch of blue, the body of a soldier crumpled up on the edge of the track, looking like a man sleeping uncomfortably, and beside him a big red stain, coagulating now. You would never think so much blood could come out of one man... A troop passes, a shell bursts, men fall. The troop cannot stop and carries on, leaving the bodies abandoned by the track. Others come by later and they cannot stop either. By then the corpses seem to be an integral part of the scene. So these sad wrecks of humanity stay there, drying, hardening or decaying little by little in their blue greatcoats and big boots, and little by little this path, which used to be pleasant, disappears under debris and dead men.'

Great clouds of flies rose at the men's approach and a heavy slaughterhouse stench caught them in the throat, adding repulsion to the atmosphere of desolation and danger. Despite its pretty name, *Bois Fleury* – Fleury Wood – was not a place to linger. The relief routes were known to the Germans, who shelled them methodically; somewhere in this area on 1 June 1916 two machine gunners in the 3rd Battalion were killed. The War Diary does not mention them but after the war grieving families placed this stone to commemorate twenty one year old *Henri Ruèche and Jacques Salamite*, who had turned twenty only the previous day. For years the stone, unreadable now, was hidden in thick undergrowth and it is thanks to the recent efforts of a local member of Souvenir Français, the French association for the perpetuation of memory, that it has been cleared and marked.

The memorial to Privates Salamite and Ruèche. *Author's collection*

A few days later two more men died in Bois Fleury, but not as a result of shelling. At 5.30pm on 11 June 1916, *Second Lieutenants Henri Herduin and Pierre Millant*, 5th Battalion, 347th Infantry, were shot without trial in this vicinity for disobeying orders to die fighting where they stood and pulling their men out of the line. The story of what happened will be told later, as it is part of the French

This memorial to Lieutenants Herduin and Millant was found by the author in bushes on the Mort-Homme in 2005. The inscription is hand written and Millant's name is incorrectly spelt. *Author's collection*

struggle to prevent the Germans from reaching the inner fortress line that involves other men remembered on this tour.

Return to your previous track and turn left uphill. Continue until you reach a hard 'white' road, then turn right **(10)** and walk ahead, noting on the left a whole series of deep excavations, some with obvious dugout entrances. They are part of the French defence of the area. After 300 metres turn right downhill between blocks 562 and 579 **(11)** and after roughly one hundred metres turn left along a level path. **Stop** when you reach a low wall on the left that surrounds a very substantial memorial. The ravine behind you is *Ravin de la Poudrière*, one of the two main French supply routes during the Battle of Verdun.

Corporal André Rachel, 3 Machine Gun Company, 167th Infantry **(12)** Corporal Rachel and his companions were casualties of the German offensive of 11 July 1916, which marks the high point of their advance.

Corporal's Rachel's extensive memorial has recently been cleared of the trees and bushes that had invaded it. *Author's collection*

The assault on Verdun progressed more slowly than General von Falkenhayn expected and, faced with the staggering cost in men and material, he was forced to consider whether it should continue. At a meeting in May 1916, the Chief of Staff of the Fifth Army, General Schmidt von Knobelsdorf, set out the stark choice they faced: to continue the offensive until they controlled certain commanding heights that dominated the

General Schmidt von Knobelsdorf. *Author's collection*

battlefield, or to withdraw across the whole front and possibly as far back as the start line of 21 February 1916. On this occasion the Commander in Chief of the Fifth Army, Crown Prince William of Germany, who had long believed that it would be difficult to achieve a decisive result at Verdun without reaching casualty levels out of all proportion with the result sought, surprised everyone by agreeing that the battle should continue until the heights were in German hands and, with the Allied operation on the Somme about to begin. there was no time to lose.

Fort Tavannes became unrecognisable after prolonged bombardment. *Author's collection*

The commanding heights in question were the hilltops occupied by Fort Souville, Fort Tavannes, the Froideterre fieldwork and the village of Fleury, and the German operation to capture them, launched on 23 June 1916, was their last throw of the dice. However, despite a massive bombardment and the use of phosgene gas, the operation failed to reach most of its objectives and at the end of the day the German lines formed

French soldiers in Fleury before the evacuation of civilians. *Author's collection*

A German trench in the Fleury sector in July 1916. *Author's collection*

a deep salient around Fleury that was under French guns on three sides. This was such an unfavourable position that on 11 July the Germans tried again. After another bombardment so massive that the ground seemed to billow like waves, elements of the Bavarian Leib Infantry broke out of the salient and fanned out across the hillside in front of you. With flame throwers and hand grenade squads in the lead, infantry and machine gunners behind, they swallowed up the machine gun post manned by *Corporal André Rachel* and captured the Poudrière [Powder Magazine] some 300 metres to your right. However, they got no further. and their

124

casualties, especially among officers, were very heavy. French casualties were heavy too. The hillside in front of you was held by the 167th Infantry and their War Diary takes sixty five pages to list the casualties of the day: almost 1500 officers and men, of whom 1329 had simply disappeared. The 167th had seven machine guns in position that day, including one which covered the railway line that ran along part of this track, so it is reasonable to assume that Rachel's gun was either on this spot or nearby. I have found no record of the names of the other men who died here with him in the terrifying noise and confusion of that day.

The broken memorial plaque to Corporal Rachel and his comrades, now clear of weeds. *Author's collection*

The Poudrière (13)

From the Rachel Memorial, continue along the track to the Poudrière, an underground ammunition magazine excavated before the First World War. Shaped roughly like a flat letter H, it had two parallel tunnels linked by a shorter third tunnel, plus various side rooms for munitions, a command post, a first aid post and a latrine. The entrance to each of the tunnels was closed by a metal door backed by an iron grille. Major Quenedy arrived here in the early hours of 1 June from the direction you have just walked:

'In front and to the right was the ravine … what devastation; in some places the shell craters overlapped and the underlying rock had been blown up so there was broken stone everywhere and everything was a sort of greyish-white. Not a tree, not a blade of grass in this infernal place, just dry sterility and arid, rocky ground... It was depressing and desolate and it smelt of destruction and death. On the left of the track a deep communication trench cut into the hillside... It led to a wooden chicane which was always full of men ... and the entrance to brigade headquarters... The brigade command post was a large underground room in the shape of an elongated rectangle. Down the middle of the room was a line of wooden posts that supported the roof. The telephone was in a corner on the left, there were tables down the right hand side and bunks at the end. The light was weak and much of the room was in shadow.'

The needs of fronts more active than Verdun meant that from October 1914 the Poudrière was progressively stripped of its ammunition and thereafter it served as a command and first aid post, supply dump and shelter. On 11 July the first group of Bavarians to reach it followed the communication trench used by Major Quenedy and found that the metal door to the western tunnel was open (this is the first entrance you see as you come from the Rachel memorial). Without fans to circulate the air, this was the only way of getting fresh air into the magazine, even though

French officers at the Poudrière in early July 1916.
Author's collection

it meant that during a bombardment the men inside had to wear gas masks for hours at a time. Quickly setting up a machine gun they opened fire into the tunnel, which was full of wounded. Minutes later, a second group armed with flame throwers reached the eastern tunnel, which housed the stretcher bearers and runners. This was too much for the men inside, whose nerves had been stretched for days by the terrifying pounding of the German heavies, and a white flag soon appeared. Far too important to be left in German hands for long, the Poudrière was recaptured in a night attack eight days later. The ruined and overgrown building next to the eastern entrance was originally the guard house.

Early photos of the guard house show a substantial building with a railway line in front of it. There is not much left of it now. *Author's collection*

Follow the track uphill to the T-junction, then turn right and continue for roughly 750 metres. **Stop** at the memorial cross on the left, just below Fleury Memorial car park **(14)**.

October 1916

The background to the deaths of the men commemorated here is the French counter offensive of 24 October 1916. Two of the men were sappers, one was a gunner, whilst the fourth was a chaplain and military nurse/orderly. All were killed by the same shell and declared dead on 25 October 1916. For more information about the counter offensive, see *Verdun – Fort Douaumont*.

127

Chaplain Alexandre Constant, 9th Division Stretcher Bearer Group
Thirty seven year old Alexandre Constant served with a stretcher bearer group that included doctors, pharmacists, dentists, an administrative officer, three Catholic chaplains and 150 men. They had arrived in Verdun on 22 October and spent an uncomfortable night in the ruins of Caserne Marceau, where the War Diary complains that they were insufficiently protected from shells exploding nearby. The next day was spent in planning evacuation routes and organising medical teams and first aid posts so that everything should be ready when the counter offensive started. Men brought to these posts were evacuated by stretcher bearers to various collection points, including one by the water tower you saw earlier. The routes were not long but they were far from easy: the 2500 metres from the first aid post at the Poudrière to the water tower involved 500 metres along a narrow communication trench, 1500 metres on difficult tracks involving a steep uphill climb from the ravine to a relay station, and finally 500 metres where a wheeled stretcher cart could be used. In theory this took an hour and fifteen minutes but in practice it could be much longer. Once at the water tower, men needing ambulance transport waited in a specially constructed shelter, while walking wounded made their own way back to Verdun – a considerable distance. As soon as the counter offensive started, all the aid posts became extremely busy and with every medical team fully occupied, they were glad to use a big batch of German prisoners with medical training who arrived during the afternoon and were put to work. Evacuation went more slowly than planned, as the artillery convoys, which used the same routes

Four men killed by the same shell. *Author's collection*

as the ambulances, took priority. As a result, the shelter by the water tower became congested and the wounded had to wait outside, where they suffered badly from cold. More than 600 men were evacuated on 24 October and the next day was just as busy but by then *Chaplain Constant* was dead; the War Diary reports that he and three other men were killed during the night of 24 – 25 October when a heavy shell fell on a dugout in a nearby fieldwork. He was posthumously awarded the Croix de Guerre and Médaille Militaire. These are the other men who died with him:

Sapper-Miner Emile Bretonnière and Sapper René Roiné, 4 Company, 11th Battalion, 6th Engineers

The early hours of 24 October 1916 saw streams of men pouring through Bois Fleury on the way to the front. They included two young sappers, twenty seven year old *Emile Bretonnière* and twenty year old *Réné Roiné*, who came up with 4 Company at 5.30am carrying two days' rations and all their tools. Three hours after the start of the counter offensive, the company was ordered forward; from groups of prisoners and wounded men heading back to French lines they learned that the objectives had been reached. Their work, which involved surveying and laying tracks, digging trenches, constructing message posts, and doing anything else needed to consolidate the gains of the day, was subject all day to violent German barrage fire, which interrupted the work and eventually lead to their deaths.

Second Lieutenant Jacques Legros, 26th Field Artillery Regiment

Jacques Legros was an observer with 2nd Battery, 26th Field Artillery Regiment, which had an advanced observation post at Fleury. The 2nd Battery was supporting troops in the Douaumont sector and on 24 October they fired over 2000 rounds, gradually lengthening the range until they were harassing German positions well beyond the final objective. The War Diary does not mention where Lieutenant Legros was serving but being only nineteen years old he may have volunteered, as did Maurice Coutier, mentioned in Tour No 3, to serve at the advanced observation post in place of older men with dependents. He was posthumously awarded the Croix de Guerre and Médaille Militaire

From here, follow the track uphill to the road (D913). A visit to Fleury Memorial museum may be convenient at this point. If not, turn right at the road and walk to the crossroads. The monument by the roadside featuring a dying Lion marks the official high water mark of the German advance in 1916.

The Lion monument marks the official high water mark of the German advance in 1916. Fort Souville is some 300 metres behind it. *Author's collection*

Ravin de Bazil and Caillette Sectors
At the crossroads, turn left downhill on the D112 for roughly 400 metres and then turn left into the wood between blocks 376 and 377. Once you get past the first major bend, look for a deep communication trench on the right. This is one of two major supply and relief routes used by regiments heading into the *Ravin de Bazil* and *Caillette* Sectors and it was not easy to negotiate, as Major Quenedy discovered in the early hours of 1 June:

'In front of me I saw a deep trench and I was glad to be on the right track. I slipped in but got out again immediately as it was full of water. About thirty metres further on it was dry, so I got back in and moved on behind the guide and another man... The trench bent left and right. It was very dark and I could just make out the sides (which I often bumped into) and the shadow of the man in front of me... After a bit we slowed down and the man in front said in a low voice 'corpse' and I spread my legs wide to get past a black shape that blocked the bottom of the trench. Then the leading man stopped. We had collided with the 2nd Battalion, which had run into a returning grenade carrying party from the 1st

Battalion. After much pushing, shoving and bumping into other men and the sides of the trench, I managed to get to the front... There were lots of bends in this part of the trench. I had to get through the branches of a tree which had fallen across it and climb over more and more bodies. There were also wounded men waiting to be picked up. Some of the grenade carrying party was there too.'

Standing close to the trench is a handsome wooden cross recently placed there by the family of twenty seven year old *Gefreiter Leonhard Sturm*, a German casualty of the battle **(15)**. Sturm, who was killed somewhere in this area on 31 July 1916, is buried in the mass grave at Hautecourt-lès-Broville, on the D603 north of Verdun.

Continue to the T-junction, then turn left between blocks 374 and 377 **(16)** and after a short distance turn right between 374 and 375 **(17)**. The track emerges into an open field and you will see the Ossuary on the left. About one hundred metres before the end of the open field, turn right into the forest again between blocks 374 and 372 and after 150 metres **(18)** turn left downhill on the *Sentier de Vaux* between 371 and 372. When you reach the valley at the bottom of the hill, **stop**. This is *Ravin de Bazil* [Bazil Ravine], a long valley of vital importance to the French because it provided access from the Woëvre Plain to the inner fortress line and thus to the heart of the Verdun defensive system. The massive slope ahead of you, hidden by trees in the summer but clearly visible in winter, is the embankment for the *Petit Meusien* light railway, which saw vicious fighting during the summer of 1916. Turn right here and follow the grassy track along the bottom of the ravine until you see a flight of steps on the left **(19)**. Climb the steps and **continue** to the top of the embankment. Face the memorial to *Lieutenant Maurice Dubuc* and his companions of the 147th Infantry who died in this area on 19 April 1916.

The recent family memorial to Leonhard Sturm. *Author's collection*

Lieutenant Maurice Dubuc's memorial on the railway embankment. *Author's collection*

131

Second Lieutenant Maurice Dubuc, 147th Infantry **(20)**
This is the Caillette Sector, a place with a terrifying reputation during the spring and summer of 1916. The steep hillside in front of you, which was wooded when the battle began, offered French observers and machine gunners camouflaged positions and controlling views over all the neighbouring sectors and forced the Germans to count their progress towards the inner fortress line in metres rather than kilometres. Sheltered access from the embankment to Fort Douaumont was provided by *Ravin de la Fausse Côte* to your right and *Ravin de la Caillette* to your left, two valleys which became the scene of terrible fighting. The German decision to continue the battle until the commanding heights were in their hands, and their need to prevent the French from recapturing Fort Douaumont, meant they had to gain control of the Caillette Sector and during the spring of 1916 – laconically referred to by one German authority as 'a period poor in progress but rich in heroism' – the fighting here made it a place of utter horror. The situation was not helped by appalling weather in April, which turned the hillside into a sodden waste of sloppy mud and collapsing trenches. Rain and continuous shelling combined to ruin every attempt to organise the position and every spade struck a corpse, adding horror and stench to cold, hunger and wet. Morale sank and troops fell ill, but slowly and with enormous effort the German lines were pushed forward until by mid-April they had captured most of *Ravin de la Fausse*

German positions in Fausse Côte ravine in the summer of 1916. *Author's collection*

French troops in Bazil Ravine. Note the steepness of the railway embankment for attacking troops. *Author's collection*

Côte and were pushing towards *Ravin de la Caillette* The aim of the operation of 19 April in which twenty year old Lieutenant Dubuc died was to recapture the new German line between the two ravines. While the battalion on the left reached its objective, Dubuc and his men, attacking on the right, were less successful. Delayed by their own artillery firing short and caught in showers of hand grenades thrown by German troops who had moved forward out of their positions to avoid the bombardment and were much closer than expected, they were forced back to their starting point, taking their neighbouring unit with them.

When withdrawn on 25 April the 147th was relieved by the 170th Infantry, a regiment known as *Les Hirondelles de la Mort* (the swallows of death), whose ranks included several Americans, former volunteers with the French Foreign Legion. One of them, Ferdinand Capdevielle, a New Yorker of French extraction, who had sailed to France to sign up in August 1914 and served through all the horrors of the Champagne battles in 1915, described the fighting in the Caillette Sector as the hardest of all. As he later wrote:

'We marched to the firing line in the dark, picking our way by the dead bodies lining the route. The Germans were shelling us to the best of their ability and our guns replied vigorously. After a stay in an almost demolished trench, we were ordered to attack the Germans. The boys were glad to be in action and covered the distance between them and the Boches in a hurry. Some of us had trench knives. Charles Hoffecker practically decapitated four Huns before he was struck by shell fragments and gravely wounded. Several of the Americans won much praise by their work.'

The 170th's aim was to retake the trenches that the Germans had recently captured, dig in, and establish solid positions with strong sentry posts overlooking Ravin de la Fausse Côte. Their efforts met a violent German response and although some progress was made it was at the cost of substantial casualties, which included several of the Americans. Among the wounded was Charles Hoffecker, who died on 3 May at the field hospital at Chaumont–sur–Aire and lies today in the French military cemetery of Rembercourt-aux-Pots, plot no 1344. He received the Medaille Militaire and Croix de Guerre and was cited in Army Orders as a valorous American volunteer, mortally wounded after killing several of the enemy in a bayonet assault against the German trenches. Ferdinand Capdevielle, who went on to survive fierce fighting at Verdun, Champagne, on the Aisne, and in the Second Battle of the Marne, was killed in October 1918. He was the last American to die in French service in the First World War and lies today in the military cemetery at Sommepy-Tahure, plot no 1025.

There are no German memorials in this sector but the cemetery in Herbebois created by Infantry Regiment 24 originally contained the bodies of three men killed here in May 1916: *Otto Drähn, Bernhard Stollbrock* and *Otto Schneidereit.* Considering the difficulties involved in transporting any casualty out of this sector while under continuous bombardment, the fact that men already dead were taken so far back for burial in the regimental cemetery implies considerable devotion to their memory and to the regiment. (See Tour No 2).

Vicefeldwebel Otto Schneidereit.
Author's collection

Bernhard Stollbrock's memorial has, alas, disappeared from the cemetery in Herbebois.
Harry van Baal

With the Dubuc memorial on your left, walk along the embankment for 250 metres. Turn left diagonally uphill between blocks 362 and 363 **(21)** and **stop** when you reach a ruined infantry shelter on the right.

Infantry Shelter DV2 **(22)**
One of the reasons for the slow German progress in the Caillette Sector was the resistance offered by French strongpoints such as this. One of four identical shelters built to accommodate infantry serving between Fort Douaumont and Fort Vaux, DV2 was built in 1906 and provided seating accommodation for a hundred men in two connecting rooms, with a kitchen in a third room and an external latrine. It was heavily shelled throughout March 1916 and attacked for the first time on 2 April, but on that occasion the Germans were thrown back.

The ruins of Infantry Shelter DV2. *Author's collection*

Strong concrete constructions like DV2 were a magnet for troops in the open and they were always full. On 17 April 1916, one of the rooms functioned as the regimental command post, while the other was a magazine and first aid post. During a particularly violent bombardment a heavy shell smashed into the entrance to the command post, burying a number of pioneers and telephonists under the rubble. The next morning there was a fire and explosion in the magazine caused, according the War Diary, 'by some unfortunate throwing away a match or cigarette'. This ignited the rockets and within seconds boxes of hand grenades began to explode. There was a wild rush to get out but the way through to the command post was obstructed by rubble, and with grenades and rockets exploding around them men panicked, trampling each other and the wounded in the effort to reach fresh air before they were suffocated. Fortunately, the explosions had also blown out some sandbags that had been used to plug a breach in the outer wall caused by the previous day's shelling, and it was through that gap that the survivors were able to escape. The result was devastating; sixteen killed and ninety three injured and burned including, in addition to doctors, stretcher bearers and nurses/orderlies, the regimental commander and his entire staff, the two battalion commanders responsible for leading the following day's assault, a battery commander, and two artillery officers who had come up for a planning meeting. An officer from a neighbouring regiment took over and, assisted by an NCO, spent the night dictating orders and trying to complete the planning for the coming day. In the circumstances it is perhaps not surprising that the following day's assault, in which Lieutenant Dubuc died, was unsuccessful.

DV2 was finally captured by the Germans on 2 June 1916 and thereafter it functioned as a relay station for runners and a place of rest for exhausted men. Being under constant observation and fire, getting in and out safely was a matter of luck and needed strong nerves. After the war Reserve Infantry Regiment 36 remembered it only too well:

'Who could forget the route from *Ravin de la Fausse Côte* to the front line through Caillette wood? French guns below Fort Souville chased us like wild animals. The memory of French trenches filled with blackened bodies, or the infantry shelter in Caillette wood that had been blown up by a German 420mm shell and was filled from floor to ceiling with corpses, still fill us with horror, but how often were we forced to take shelter there? Anyone who managed to get back [to the ravine] without being wounded breathed a sigh of relief.'

The French only recaptured DV2 on 24 October 1916. To see what it looked like before it was ruined, visit Infantry Shelter FT1 (PC 120), which is signposted off the slip road leading to the *Ouvrage de Froideterre*.

Continue uphill, noting the many trenches and positions to be seen on both sides of the track. When you reach the T-junction with a hard, sandy track (*Chemin d'Hardaumont*) turn left downhill and **stop** at the recently restored memorial to *Private Paul Sommières*, 2 Machine Gun Company, 75th Infantry, who died somewhere in this area on 5 June 1916 **(23)**. The

Before it was smashed, DV2 looked like this: Infantry Shelter FT1, also known as PC120, close to the Ouvrage de Froideterre. *Author's collection*

story of what happened to Private Sommières and his companions will be told later. Continue downhill to the T-junction with the railway embankment, then turn right and continue for approximately a hundred metres until you reach the memorial to *Jacques Louis Lyon*, holder of the Croix de Guerre and Légion d'Honneur, which stands on the left among fir trees below the level of the embankment **(24)**. Walk down to the memorial and face the ravine.

The Sommières memorial. *Author's collection*

Ravin de Bazil is captured
On 22 May 1916 the French did what the Germans had feared they would do: they tried to recapture Fort Douaumont. Although unsuccessful, the attempt led the Germans to redouble their efforts to push French lines away from the fort and secure it from surprise attack. The French regiment which took over after the failure was the 24th Infantry, which came up on 25 May and took up position with all three battalions in line. Fighting in this sector had been continuous since early April and by the end of May the everlasting

German stretcher bearers in Fausse Côte Ravine under the protection of a Red Cross flag. *Tom Gudmestad*

bombardment had destroyed the woodland and wiped out every trace of organisation, leaving men on both sides crouching without shelter in a horrible wasteland of shell holes and trying as best they could to maintain liaison to left and right. By the end of May, 1200 men had been killed or wounded, companies had been reduced to a scattering of men in shell craters, there was no organised line and only one machine gun remained in action. At 4am on 1 June, following a particularly devastating barrage of gas and high explosive, dense masses of German troops fell on the whole French line and while it held on the left, it broke in the Caillette Sector. German troops, led by a specially trained unit from Sturm-Bataillon Rohr headed by flamethrowers and hand grenade squads, smashed into what was left of the 24th Infantry, surrounded them, and swarmed on to the railway line, where they invaded the regimental command post. Only a handful of men managed to get back through the barrage to bring the news that the French line had been breached and that the 24th was destroyed. In their War Diary the entry for 1 June reads: '3.30am. Violent bombardment of our first line and a zone approximately one kilometre to the rear. Since then, no news of the regiment. Casualty figures for the day: 1728.' A captain took command of what was left – ration parties, cooks, drivers and the few survivors of the assault.

Private Saint-Just Borical, 119th Infantry
The destruction of the 24th Infantry left a gaping hole in the French line and, in an effort to prevent the Germans from exploiting it, several units were rushed forward on 1 June. These included the 119th Infantry, which

was previously met in Bois Fleury. The urgency of the situation meant that they had to move up in broad daylight despite a terrifying bombardment; but by the time they reached their positions the Germans were firmly established on the embankment and well supplied with machine guns. Unable to advance, the 119th dug in at the top of the hill on the other side of the ravine and waited for the signal to attack. It came at 2am on 3 June. With grenadiers in the lead, three waves of men from the 1st and 2nd battalions launched an assault on the embankment but they were mown down by machine-gun fire and got nowhere. The Germans counter attacked immediately but somehow the French line held and each side remained where it was. When the 119th was relieved on 7 June the regiment had lost 734 men, 248 of whom had simply disappeared.

One of the men missing on 3 June was twenty-nine year old *Private Saint-Just Louis Borical*. He was born in Cayenne, the capital of Guyane (Guiana), which was then a French colony on the coast of South America and part of a vast colonial empire, consisting of territories in Africa, Asia and the Pacific. Borical had been a sailor, most probably in the coastal trade, until 20 August 1915, when he was examined, judged fit for military service and sent to France.

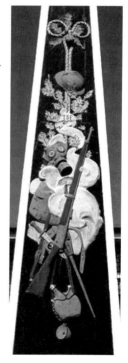

Arriving there in September, he and other Creole soldiers were sent to Algeria for training, and it was on his return to France in May 1916 that he joined the 119th. He was not alone: nine other Guyanese soldiers joined the regiment with him, all heading to the front line for the first time in the unimaginable violence of June 1916.

Private Borical was declared dead on 13 June 1916 and his remains were only found in April 2011. The War Diary only mentions officers by name and the precise circumstances of his death are unknown; but from where his remains were found it seems likely that he died in the failed counter attack. If so, he is one of the 178 men declared missing that day. He was quickly identified and posthumously decorated with the Médaille Militaire and Croix de Guerre with bronze star. The accompanying citation described him as a courageous and devoted soldier, who fell gloriously on the field of honour on 3 June 1916 at Fleury while valiantly performing his duty. No family could be

A gas mask, French helmet, rifle, canteen and cup are among the First World War subjects on this war memorial in Cayenne. *Marie-Odile and Philippe Delaunay*

Private Borical was welcomed home to Cayenne with a state funeral. The inscription on his gravestone in Guyanese Creole reads: 'Saint-Just Borical, a son of Guyane, born at Cayenne, the people of this country are happy to be by your side and wish that you may rest in peace.' *Marie-Odile and Philippe Delaunay*

found but the city of Cayenne welcomed their returning son with full military honours.

The cemetery in front of the Ossuary contains the remains of another decorated soldier from Cayenne who also served in a line regiment. *Corporal Augustin Thébia*, 102nd Infantry, died somewhere between Fleury and the Thiaumont fieldwork on 3 September 1916 and is buried in plot 2566. The citation describes him as an 'Energetic corporal of admirable devotion to duty. His attitude under fire was particularly brilliant in the attack on the village of Fleury in which he led his squad towards the enemy and was killed.'

Second Lieutenant Jacques Louis Lyon, 119th Infantry
Lieutenant Lyon died in the same assault as Private Borical but, being an officer, the War Diary mentions him by name. A plaque on a substantial family memorial in Père Lachaise Cemetery, Paris, describes him as having taken part in the 1914 battles of Charleroi, Guise and the Marne, which involved an 800 kilometre march. Promoted to sergeant in 1915 and to second lieutenant in January 1916, Jacques Lyon had received two citations for volunteering to carry out reconnaissance missions in February and March 1916; and it was on another such voluntary mission that he met his death.

Lieutenant Jacques Louis Lyon and his memorial. *Author's collection*

Now return to the top of the embankment and walk the short distance to the next junction. Face back the way you have come. *Ravin de la Caillette* is on your left.

Private Paul Sommières, 75th Infantry Regiment
Private Sommières, whose memorial you saw on the *Chemin d'Hardaumont*, was a machine gunner with the 2nd Battalion, 75th Infantry, when they attacked alongside Borical's regiment on 3 June. The German assault of 1 June which destroyed the 24th Infantry had left a

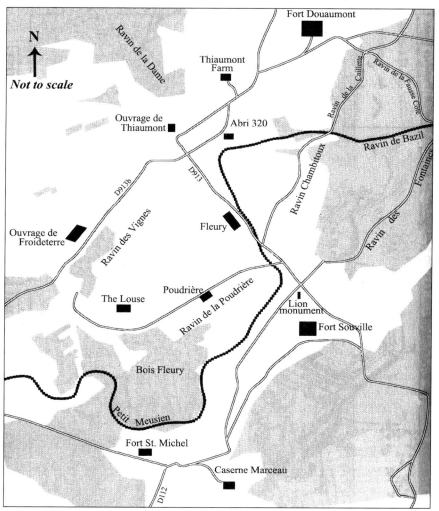

Forests and cleared areas in the central sector of the Right Bank in 1916.

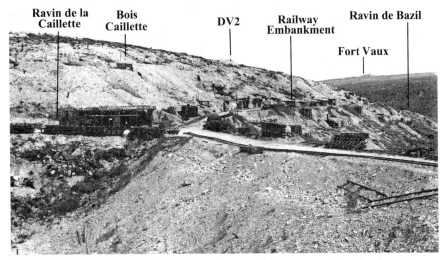

Ravin de la Caillette   Bois Caillette   DV2   Railway Embankment   Ravin de Bazil

Fort Vaux

Plans of the 75th Infantry positions show machine guns on the embankment approximately at the junction with the Ravin de la Caillette. Note the commanding position of DV2 on the bare hillside and Fort Vaux on the horizon to the right.

gap of several hundred metres in the French line, and the 2nd Battalion, 75th Infantry, was ordered forward to fill it. They had a difficult time getting into line. Held up in Bois Fleury close to a 75mm battery that was attracting attention from German gunners, they suffered numerous casualties, whilst their route forward brought them along the railway embankment in bright daylight and within sight of German machine guns. One by one, and taking shelter wherever they could, the 2nd Battalion finally managed to get into some sort of position across the embankment here but the situation was completely chaotic; there was no liaison to left or right and the whereabouts of the 119th were unknown. At 2am on 3 June two companies from the 2nd Battalion, supported by machine gunners, moved off with orders to retake a commanding position known as the *Signal de la Caillette* and to block a further German advance along the embankment. They made some progress at first but ran into a wall of machine-gun fire and got no further. A second attempt planned for 9am the same day was abandoned and it was nightfall before the reserves could come up, locate the 119th and establish liaison. There was no organised front line; the ground was so devastated that it was impossible to create a support line and, with the men scattered here and there in shell craters, no further operations could be attempted.

The 75th lost almost 150 men on 3 June. They should have been relieved that night but the front was so chaotic that they could only be withdrawn gradually in small groups and the machine gunners had to stay put until 7 June. By then, *Paul Sommières* was dead. The circumstances of his death are unknown; but the machine gunners were in the most exposed position and while waiting to be relieved they suffered from continuous bombardment. Private Sommières was a native of Mende, Lozère Department and in addition to the handsome memorial you saw earlier, which stands close to the *Signal de la Caillette*, he is commemorated in the recently established *Fôret des Poilus*, where a tree has been planted in the name of each man from Mende who fell during the First World War.

A squad of machine gunners from the 100th Infantry with a Hotchkiss machine gun on the right and a St. Etienne on the left. Note the range finder held by the gunner on the back row. The 100th Infantry was involved in hard fighting for the Poudriere in July 1916. *Tom Gudmestad*

Now continue along the embankment. After just over one kilometre turn right uphill along a sandy track to Abri 320 **(25)**. Stand by the first of the 'chimneys' and face across the valley.

Shot without trial: Second Lieutenants Henri Herduin and Pierre Millant, 347th Infantry
During the Battle of Verdun the long underground shelter beneath your feet was known as the Thiaumont Redoubt. It was originally designed to house reserves but during the violent summer of 1916 it served as a

Abri 320 is a 70 metres long brick lined cavern originally constructed to offer safe underground shelter to reserves. It is inaccessible. This is a view inside Four Chimneys Shelter below the Ouvrage de Froideterre, which is an identical construction. *Author's collection*

command post and general refuge. At that time the German thrust in this sector was coming from left to right and one of the regiments to feel the full force of it was the 347th Infantry, a reserve regiment of two battalions (5th and 6th) which had been serving in a quiet sector for more than a year. During the night of 4-5 June, the 5th Battalion was ordered up to Bois Fleury, where two companies (17 and 19) were ordered to take position in front of Thiaumont Farm. This was a cluster of buildings, now disappeared, forming a strongpoint on high ground roughly one kilometre from Fort Douaumont and close to where the *Abri des Pèlerins* café/restaurant stands today. The battalion's other two companies followed the next day. At that time the French front in this sector ran, roughly speaking, from Thiaumont Farm down the hillside to your left, across the railway embankment, through *Ravin de Bazil* and up the hillside facing you. The regimental command post was here in the redoubt.

Despite receiving sketch maps showing organized trenches, the 5th Battalion's position proved to be just a series of muddy craters, where every movement could be seen by observers on the ground or in the air. Their attempts to organize it were prevented by a thundering bombardment that reduced visibility, cut the phone lines as fast as they could be mended, broke up communications, and prevented runners and ration parties from getting through. By 8 June the position was completely disorganised and, with no front line, few men, and weapons coated with mud, there was little the 5th Battalion could do when a strong force of German troops, fired up by the previous day's surrender of Fort Vaux, surged towards them and overran the battalion command post. At 12.30pm on 8 June the regiment's colonel informed brigade that he was out of contact with the 5th Battalion and that the bombardment of the redoubt was so heavy that runners could neither get in nor out. The 6th Battalion was ordered forward but furious shelling prevented them from getting into position. During the afternoon the Germans reached this redoubt and in violent fighting attack after attack was repelled but the colonel was killed. When night fell the 6th Battalion, which had started the day 600 strong, was down to eight officers and 190 men; the 5th Battalion had disappeared and there was a yawning gap in the line. The gap was only closed on 9 June and when the stunned remnants of the 347th returned to Bois Fleury the casualty list ran to almost 2000 names. It included many from the 5th Battalion but there were a few survivors and, to everyone's surprise, some of them turned out to be in Verdun.

According to the War Diary of 103 Brigade, on 11 June the 347th's acting commander, Captain Delaruelle, was informed that elements of 17 and 19 Companies commanded by *Second Lieutenants Herduin and Millant* had abandoned Thiaumont Farm despite formal orders to the contrary and were currently in Verdun. Speaking to their comrades, Herduin and Millant explained that when night fell on 8 June 1916 most of their men were dead, they were out of food and ammunition, and threatened with encirclement; under the cover of darkness a group of about forty men withdrew from the line, taking their equipment and eight machine guns. They first tried to join a neighbouring regiment but the commander refused to accept them and ordered them back to their positions. They then continued to Verdun, where the two lieutenants were reported to brigade and divisional commanders. Everyone was stunned. There was no doubt that their action was directly contrary to orders. The Commander-in-Chief, General Joffre, and the Second Army Commander, General Nivelle, had both ordered

Lieutenant Herduin.
Author's collection

General Nivelle.
Author's collection

145

The destruction of the Meuse bridges was a German objective during the Battle of Verdun. This is the Pont de la Galavaude in central Verdun. *Author's collection*

the high ground on the Right Bank to be held at all costs to prevent the Germans from threatening the Meuse bridges; only a week earlier General Nivelle had written to his commanders informing them that 'we should not take so much as one step back ... even if that means we must die where we stand'. If the Right Bank fell, Verdun would have to be abandoned and that could not be contemplated, particularly just before the Allied offensive on the Somme. General Headquarters had recently received reports of a crisis of moral at Verdun and 'acts of indiscipline', which included men refusing to go forward, excuses accepted by their officers, and only minor sanctions imposed. In the circumstances it was vital that discipline be restored immediately. Without giving the two lieutenants a chance to explain themselves, Captain Delaruelle ordered them back to Bois Fleury. The divisional commander ordered them to be shot. The 347th's war diary is brief and to the point:

'5pm: Order no 1101 from Colonel Commanding 103 Brigade: Second Lieutenant Herduin, 17 Company, 347th Infantry Regiment, and Second Lieutenant Millant, 19 Company. 347th Infantry, who left the field of battle without orders, abandoning the fight, have committed a crime. They are to be shot on receipt of this order.

5.30pm: Order no 1102 from Colonel Commanding 103 Brigade: The two officers are to be shot. Immediate execution.

5.43pm: In accordance with the orders received, Second Lieutenants Herduin and Millant were executed at 5.43pm. They behaved with dignity. The coup de grâce was given to both men.'

Discipline was restored, but the men were not forgotten.

From here, return to the railway embankment, turn right and continue to the D913. Cross the road to the memorial to the *5ième Regiment d'Artillerie à Pied*, a heavy artillery regiment forming part of the Verdun garrison. The broken gun barrel lying behind it is the same calibre as the guns shown on the memorial. Turn right and walk along the D913 to the site of the destroyed village of Fleury, one of nine villages on the battlefield considered to have died for France. There is information about the village on the signboards by the path to the chapel. For more information on the fighting in this area, see *Walking Verdun*.

The memorial to the 5ième régiment d'artillerie à pied, one of the Verdun garrison regiments. The regiment had eleven batteries serving the artillery in the Verdun forts and a further two serving the fortress of Longwy. *Author's collection*

Fleury-devant-Douaumont

In August 1914 this was a small farming village of three streets whose most recent excitement had been the arrival of the *Petit Meusien* railway a few months earlier. However, once the battle began Fleury took on an importance out of all proportion to its size because it stood in the centre

of a long crest that linked the two most heavily
fortified ridges on the Right Bank and provided
gunners and observers with extensive views over
German movements and supply ravines. As a result,
it was soon surrounded by a complex defensive
system, which included batteries, trenches, dugouts
and fieldworks. The Germans captured most of
Fleury on 23 June 1916 and cleared the French out
of the remainder on 11 July, but the French were
determined to get it back and, after a month of
effort, they succeeded. The Germans were driven
back across the D913, where they remained until
October 1916. The continuing artillery battle
crushed the houses to powder and they have never
been rebuilt.

The wooden poilu who
guards the place where
twenty six French
soldiers were found in
2013. Sadly, the bayonet
has recently been broken
off. *Author's collection*

Walk down the path towards the chapel. About half
way down on the right a footpath under the trees
leads to a wooden sculpture of a French soldier,
who guards the place where bones were seen in
May 2013. Careful excavation revealed the remains
of twenty-six French soldiers whose bodies had
been placed in the cellar of an old farm to await
burial. Seven could be identified and three families
were traced. Two of the men were returned to their
places of origin and the others were buried in front of the Ossuary in a
formal ceremony held in December 2013. They lie in plots 538 – 524.

Fleury War Memorial; Memorial to Herduin and Millant
Visit the chapel, then walk back up the path and turn right toward the
village war memorial. Four of the eight men listed were born in Fleury,
including the two Ligonys, Léon Lehallé and Léon Poncet. Born in 1883,
Alphonse Ligony was the eldest, with the two *Léons and Camille Ligony*
all coming between September 1887 and November 1888. They would
have known one another all their lives. Léon Poncet and Camille Ligony
served in the 151st Infantry, one of the Verdun regiments, and Léon's
death in November 1914, the first of the eight recorded here, must have
brought war home to Fleury with shocking force.

Very different in style is the recent memorial to *Lieutenants Herduin and
Millant* **(26)**, which was inaugurated in 2006. An enquiry held after the
war found that the two lieutenants should have been allowed to explain

There are clear signs of shelling on the hillside behind the memorial in this old view. Note the touring car just visible at the top of the bank on the left. *Author's collection*

themselves to their superior officers, and they were posthumously rehabilitated. In 1919 both bodies were exhumed; Herduin was reburied in the family plot in Rheims, while Millant lies in plot 6177 in front of the Ossuary. But strong feelings remained, and ninety years after the execution the idea of commemorating two men who had disobeyed orders gave rise locally to considerable argument. On mobilization in 1914, thirty-six year old Herduin was an adjutant with fifteen years' experience in the army, including eleven years on campaign, a military medal and a China campaign medal. Millant, aged 30, had already won the Croix de Guerre. Why men of such proven experience and valour should have abandoned the line, presumably knowing the consequences of their actions, remains a mystery. The men they took with them rejoined their units without sanction; but a few days later the 347th Infantry was disbanded and the remnants incorporated into the 348th. A few days later 103 Brigade was also disbanded.

The memorial to Lieutenants Herduin and Millant inaugurated in 2006. *Author's collection*

149

The Louse **(27)**

From here, follow the wide grassy track past the wooden barrier towards the *Ravin des Vignes*. Continue for roughly 1500 metres and **stop** when you reach an area of mown grass and low trenches on the left. **Face ahead**. This is the only easily accessible part of a French fieldwork whose importance is impossible to understand today because trees block the views in all directions. During the Battle of Verdun these were bare hillsides and this fieldwork commanded both of the main French supply ravines in this area – *Ravin de la Poudrière* ahead of you and *Ravin de Vignes* to your right. It also communicated directly with Fort Souville, Fort St. Michel, Fort Belleville and the Froideterre fieldwork. A substantial earthwork of roughly oval shape, some 200 metres long and crisscrossed with trenches, it was officially called the *Ouvrage du Bois Fleury*; but its shape meant that for lice-ridden troops on both sides it was simply The Louse.

During the German offensive of 11 July 1916, a small group of enterprising Bavarians decided to try their luck here even though it was not officially one of their objectives. Arriving at the eastern end unnoticed in the confusion of the battle, they captured two machine guns and their crews and stormed on, yelling and shouting as if leading a mass assault. The Louse was defended by a handful of gassed, confused and exhausted men from the 168th Infantry, who were completely taken by surprise and, when the leader of the little group of attackers shouted in French that they were surrounded, they quickly surrendered. Backed by the captured machine guns, the leader of the assault party then went through the

An aerial view of the fieldwork known as The Louse. *Author's collection*

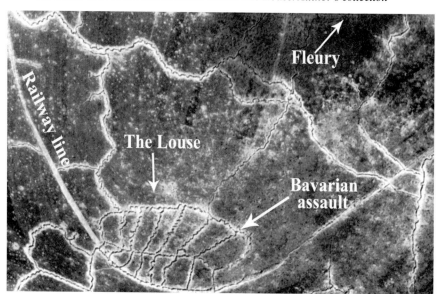

dugouts, threatening the defenders with flamethrowers until everyone was rounded up. One officer and seventy men were triumphantly marched back to German lines, where they were met by applause and loud shouts of 'Hurrah!' Later in the day the Louse was reoccupied by the 168th and it remained in French hands thereafter. Together with the Lion Monument at the crossroads by Fleury Memorial, this fieldwork marks the high point of the German advance in the Battle of Verdun.

Now carry on downhill to the *Chemin de la Poudrière*. Following your previous route, turn left at the T-junction, continue for 300 metres and turn right downhill between blocks 562 and 579. Follow the track down into *Ravin de la Poudrière*, cross the ravine, which is likely to be wet, and continue uphill until you reach the T-junction with the railway embankment. Turn left between 567 and 561 and after roughly one hundred metres turn right directly uphill between blocks 566 and 565 **(28)**. At the road (D112), turn right to return to the picnic site.

GPS Waypoints Tour 4

1. N49°08.821' E005°05.026'
2. N49°19.544' E005°25.528'
3. N49°10.633' E005°24.431'
4. N49°10.857' E005°24.614'
5. N49°10.773' E005°24.681'
6. N49°11.001' E005°24.907'
7. N49°11.103' E005°24.724'
8. N49°11.155' E005°24.802'
9. N49°11.189' E005°24.753'
10. N49°11.264' E005°24.879'
11. N49°11.332' E005°25.098'
12. N49°11.330' E005°25.256'
13. N49°11.404' E005°25.465'
14. N49°11.655' E005°26.041'
15. N49°11.765' E005°26.625'
16. N49°11.914' E005°26.448'
17. N49°11.915' E005°26.385'
18. N49°12.147' E005°26.593'
19. N49°12.358' E005°27.089'
20. N49°12.417' E005°27.093'
21. N49°12.454' E005°27.299'
22. N49°12.546' E005°27.028'

23. N49°12.535' E005°26.614'
24. N49°12.402' E005°26.477'
25. N49°12.321' E005°25.759'
26. N49°11.825' E005°25.774'
27. N49°11.348' E005°24.837'
28. N49°11.096' E005°25.460'

Other Waypoints Related to the Tour

Church of St Jean Baptiste, Avenue de la 43ième Division, Verdun:
N49°09.792' E005°23.603'

Faubourg Pavé cemetery, Avenue Maréchal Joffre:
N49°09.849' E005°24.289'

Aftermath

In 1922, Jean Norton Cru, a fluent English-speaker who had served in the French army throughout the war and later achieved fame as the author of *Témoins* (Witnesses), a critical analysis of every French war memoir published between 1915 and 1928, returned to Verdun on a pilgrimage. For three days he walked the former battlefield visiting, first, those sectors of the Right Bank closest to Verdun, then Cote 304, the Mort-Homme, Malancourt and Montfaucon on the Left Bank, and lastly Bezonvaux, Ornes, Louvemont and Bras. Having served in those sectors between October 1914 and January 1917, he now saw the battlefield again, four years after the cyclone had passed.

'My impression? Indescribable, tremendous, incredible – it surpasses all I could have imagined. And it is unique, rare, for if there are crowds of French and foreign tourists at Verdun, they make the whole classic tour by automobile over the fine road built along the line of the forts. But I have gone beyond, where the battle remains congealed amidst the ruins, over ground covered with tangles of barbed wire and briers, encumbered

This unusual German post war view shows a damaged French battery close to the former site of Bellevue Farm. Note the touring car in the background.
Tom Gudmestad

with all the wreckage of battle, full of unexploded shells, of grenades ready to go off ... nobody goes there; it is thick undergrowth, treacherous, hiding enormous shell holes full of water. A silence of death reigns there ... suddenly interrupted by the sharp bursting of a shell, then another, and yet another, accompanied by the whistle of the flying fragments. I asked myself if in this resurrection of souvenirs of a dead past, very dead, I was not subject to a hallucination. No, the shells are real. In certain unfrequented ravines a small crew of engineers hunt out unexploded shells, throw them into a big shell crater, and set them off by means of a detonator. All this forward section is such as it was left at the armistice. The villages of Fleury, Vaux, Louvemont, Ornes, Douaumont, Cumières will not be rebuilt. The ground is dispossessed. Not only does nothing of the villages remain, but the earth has been destroyed. Before building, before clearing away, it would be necessary to create an artificial surface of soil. And the main point is that this is exactly what the visitors do not see. To see it, it would be necessary to do what I have done, strike out at a venture though one knew the terrain, to be on guard against traps, push through an impossible jungle, subject oneself to great fatigue, and go without eating to reach at last the true Verdun, that of the battle, that which still speaks by a thousand signs of all that was the year 1916 ....'

With the scenes described by Jean Norton Cru repeated along the length of the Western Front, the task of returning the former battlefields to agricultural, industrial and urban use was gigantic. In France preparation for it began in 1917 with the establishment of the *Ministère des Régions libérées* [Ministry for the Liberated Regions], which divided the front into three sectors on the basis of the damage suffered. The first was the zone of passage or occupation, where there was little destruction and the land could be returned to agricultural or pre-war use after the clearance of debris; this was coloured blue on the map. The second was the zone of operations, where there was more damage and considerable restoration work would be required; this was coloured yellow. The third was the area of greatest devastation, where everything was destroyed and all traces of pre-war life had been swept away. Coloured red on the map, this was the area where the cost of rehabilitation was greater than the land was worth. It became known as the Red Zone and in the Verdun area it covered much of the former battlefield.

Les villages détruits – The destroyed villages
The first people to return to their former homes in the Red Zone naturally wished to clear the ground and rebuild; but the devastation was so great, and the dangers and difficulties so overwhelming, that after consulting

A typical view near Ornes after the battle. *Wim Degrande*

the landowners the government undertook to purchase those areas where restoration to pre-war use would involve excessive expense.

At Verdun this included nine municipalities in which the destruction of houses, farms, fields and forests made them impossible to restore. The villages of Beaumont, Fleury, Douaumont and Vaux-devant-Damloup, Bezonvaux, Ornes, Louvemont, Haumont and Cumières, all annihilated during 1916, were never rebuilt and are regarded as having died for

The site of Fleury after the Battle of Verdun. No one would ever know that a village had stood here. *Tom Gudmestad*

France. Despite that, they have retained an administrative existence. On each site there is a chapel dedicated to the patron saint of the village, a war memorial and a cemetery; descendants of families registered as living in the village before the outbreak of war may be married in the chapel or buried in the cemetery, and Mass is said there annually on the feast day of the patron saint. Each destroyed village also has a mayor with a small budget who, assisted by two councillors, takes decisions concerning the site and maintains the war memorial and the cemetery. Some sites, such as Fleury, Haumont and Bezonvaux, have been partially cleared; paths have been laid out and there are benches, information boards and explanations about life before the First World War. However, not every site can be treated in this way. The old village of Vaux-devant-Damloup stood alongside a deep stream and shelling turned the whole area into a marsh. The new village, which grew up after the war around the station serving the *Petit Meusien* light railway, stands on a new site outside the Red Zone. At Ornes there is also a cluster of houses just outside the Red Zone. Apart from a couple of hunters' cabins, the only post-war buildings in the Red Zone are Fleury Memorial museum, the Ossuary and the buildings housing its staff, and the *Abri des Pèlerins* café/restaurant.

Destruction at Ornes. *Wim Degrande*

Having decided on expropriation, the next question was what should be done with the land? Before the war the economy of the Verdun region had been based on forestry and agriculture – there were several sizeable military garrisons to supply and feed, after all – but farms, fields and drainage systems had been destroyed, while forests, if they still existed

The impressive war memorial at Ornes commemorates forty nine men who died in the war, as well as three civilians who were shot and two children killed by shelling. *Author's collection*

at all, had been reduced by wartime use to a fraction of their former size. Despite that, the general feeling was that a place where so many men had died could not simply be abandoned and eventually, after many years of sometimes acrimonious discussion and argument, it was decided that the best option was to clear the battlefield of debris and human remains and then plant trees.

Reconstitution of the forests
In the Meuse department, where two thirds of the pre-war forests had been damaged or destroyed, a forestry reconstitution service was established in 1919 with the aim of clearing the debris and replanting. This involved tearing up hundreds of kilometres of wire, filling in and levelling the trenches, and removing tons of metal of one sort or another. It immediately became clear that the cost of levelling the trenches was far more than the task was worth and it was decided – fortunately for today's visitor – to limit the work to what was strictly necessary. As a result, trenches were only filled in where tracks and paths were needed; otherwise the surface was left as it was. Even so, it was an enormous task.

Destruction of the forest between Fort Tavannes and Fort Souville. *Author's collection*

The army took away and destroyed shells and ammunition, while the forestry department supervised the recovery of wood from huts, mines and dugouts and the recovery of non-explosive metal debris was contracted out to specialized firms under supervision. It was a dangerous task and there were numerous accidents, including fatal ones. Human remains, sometimes identifiable but often just bones and scraps of cloth, were also found and removed.

In April 1923, the government entrusted the reforestation of the Red Zone on both sides of the River Meuse to the *Administration des Eaux et Forêts*. However, it was 1927 before the battlefields were sufficiently cleared of human and material debris for the work to begin; and by then spontaneous regeneration had resulted in a thick mass of vegetation. Planting, which was done by hand, was a difficult and time-consuming operation carried out by teams of local and foreign labourers, often by women. Between 1927 and 1935 thirty-six million trees were planted in parts of the Red Zone that could not be returned to agriculture or used for military training, while certain areas of particular historical importance were preserved. These included the central sector of the battlefield, where the Ossuary stands today, Fort Douaumont, Fort Vaux, the Butte de Vauquois, and the Krupp gun position in Bois de

**The ammunition bunkers in the Krupp gun position in Bois de Warphemont.
Light railway lines run into the tunnels.** *Author's collection*

Warphemont, which was the target of the 164mm naval gun in Herbebois
(see Walk No 2). The first plantings involved pines, spruces and firs,
which grew well in poor soil; but oak, silver birch and maple were also
planted, with ash, elder and poplars in the valley bottoms. Gradually the
pines, which helped to reconstitute the soil but proved ill adapted to local
conditions, have been replaced by deciduous trees, including beeches,
which are better suited to the climate and the soil. Some areas of the Red
Zone have never been reforested and the trees and bushes there today –
natural regrowth from pre-war vegetation which, while dense, is often of
poor quality – are an important source of study for botanists and
ecologists.

Returning the fallen
Within a few days of the start of the war families were asking for the
bodies of their loved ones to be returned. This had not been the practice
in earlier wars, and in 1915 the return of bodies was prohibited, because
the task of transporting human remains from the front to all parts of
France was too much for a country at war. To lessen the disappointment,
a law was passed giving the right to a perpetual resting place on French
soil to any soldier who died for France. While this situation was
grudgingly accepted during the war, the refusal of the French government
to allow bodies to be returned after the Armistice provoked
incomprehension and distress, and the government came under growing
pressure to raise the prohibition. A campaign led by members of

Temporary accommodation for workers clearing the battlefields, many of them foreign. *Tom Gudmestad*

parliament and leading army officers who had lost sons at the front, supported by the press, resulted in a proposal for a law that would not only allow the bodies to be returned but would do so at government expense. This would ensure the equal treatment of all grieving families, whether rich or poor. After eight months of argument and debate, the law was adopted: the government undertook to cover the expenses of exhumation, identification, transfer to a hermetically sealed coffin, transport from the place of exhumation to the place of reburial, and the reburial itself. The travelling expenses of certain family members who wished to be present at the exhumation were also covered. However, the right to request the return of a body was limited to wives, parents and children of the deceased, and this caused some distress in families where the only remaining relatives were siblings. Inevitably, there were disagreements over whether or not a body should be returned – parents perhaps wanting their son back, while his widow preferred him to remain with his former comrades.

The government regarded the return of the fallen as a moral duty; it was not limited to officers but applied to all men equally on the ground that where there was equality of sacrifice, there must be equality of treatment. In previous conflicts only the bodies of kings, or of wealthy or celebrated men, had been returned to France, so this was a novel idea that symbolized the gratitude of the Nation towards all those whose blood had been shed for it. However, the law only concerned those who were officially declared *Mort pour la France* between 2 August 1914 and 24 October 1919, so it did not apply to men who had died in prison or been shot as an example to others, and at first it did not cover men who died in prisoner of war camps, although this was later changed. Return requests had to be made before February 1921, although there were

160

A post war cemetery in the Verdun sector. Establishing them near railway lines facilitated the transport of remains. *Tom Gudmestad*

special rules for bodies identified after that date. Within a few years, the remains of roughly 250,000 men had been returned to their families.

Exhuming the dead
If the return of so many men from different parts of the front (and later from other countries) to towns and villages across France was an enormous task, demanding careful organization, so also was the exhumation and reburial of the men whose bodies were not returned but regrouped in national cemeteries or ossuaries maintained by the *Ministère des Pensions*. There are nineteen such cemeteries at Verdun. A special government department, the *Service de la Restitution des corps*, was set

Provisional Ossuary   Fort Douaumont

Until the Ossuary was built, the scattered bones recovered from the battlefield were housed in this provisional shelter. *Author's collection*

A view inside the provisional Ossuary. The bones were placed in containers corresponding to the sector where they were found and Mass was said every day. *Author's collection*

up to organize their exhumation, identification, transport and reburial, and the work was awarded by tender to a small number of private contractors. With 960,000 bodies exhumed by the end of 1925, the contracts proved to be very lucrative; but they were also open to abuse because, rather than receiving a fixed sum for a defined contract, contractors and labourers were remunerated on the basis of the number of separate operations carried out. There were allegations of single bodies being split between several coffins in order to make more money, of personal possessions being stolen, and even of French and German remains being mixed up and buried together. The press had been revealing such practices for several years when in 1926 a scandal broke that shocked everyone. In 1922 the contract for clearing a wartime cemetery in the Champagne region containing 950 French and German bodies had been given to one of the private contractors, who was paid to exhume the remains and reinter them elsewhere. The land was handed back to the owner and an area formerly containing sixty graves was then sold for building, but when the labourers began to dig they immediately found bones. Investigations revealed that, in that one section alone, most of the graves still contained either bones or exhumation debris, two bodies were still in situ, a third body was headless, and there were identity discs in the graves of men who had been buried as unknown. Accusations of bribery and corruption, reaching to the highest levels, led to more official investigations that brought other shocking details to light: bodies forgotten, damaged or mixed up, bones smashed by spades, skulls left in piles, bodies with too many hands or no feet, or coffins weighted with extra boots or soil. The private contractors were dismissed and the government took over – at a much lower cost. If it was a scandal that certain private contractors should have enriched themselves at the expense of the men who died for France, it was also a source of deep sorrow for the families, some of whom could no longer be sure that the body bearing the name of their son, husband or father really was who it was supposed to be.

The case of Charles Rudrauf
The search for human remains was officially called off in 1935. A recent investigation into the case of Charles (or Karl) Rudrauf, an Alsatian soldier with three graves in the Verdun area, shows how impossible it was to get everything right every time. Charles, who was mobilized in the German army and killed at Verdun on 3 August 1916, was exhumed from his provisional resting place after the war and reburied by a French burial party in the German cemetery at Romagne-sous-les-Côtes. However, his family, who regarded themselves as French, asked for his body to be exhumed again and buried as *Mort pour la France* in the French military cemetery at Mangiennes, a village close to Romagne. The tale of his exhumation twists and turns between Romagne, a new cemetery in Mangiennes, of which all trace has disappeared, the existing French and German cemeteries in that village, and finally the French military cemetery at Pierrepont where, as Charles Rudrauf, he was finally reinterred on 15 March 1926. However, Karl Rudrauf has a grave in the German cemetery at Mangiennes and also – despite the exhumation – another one at Romagne, and no one knows whose sons lie there. In reality, all one can hope is that, whoever they are, they are finally at peace.

Two of Charles Rudrauf's three graves: German in Romagne-sous-les-Côtes and French in Pierrepont.
Pierre Lenhard

German cemeteries

After the war, the position regarding German cemeteries was governed by Article 224 of the Versailles Treaty, under which the Allied and Associated (for example, the USA was an 'associate' power) governments agreed with the German government that the graves of soldiers and sailors buried in their respective territories would be respected and maintained. The German government also agreed to recognise any commission appointed by an Allied or Associated government for the purpose of identifying, registering, caring for, or erecting, suitable memorials over the graves, and to facilitate its work. That left Germany powerless in the matter of battlefield clearance, the exhumation of field graves and provisional cemeteries, the extension of existing cemeteries, and the creation of new ones. In the years immediately following the Armistice it was French contractors who cleared the German battlefield cemeteries and field graves and reinterred the remains elsewhere; it was only gradually that the *Volksbund Deutsche Kriegsgräberfürsorge*, a body originally set up in 1919, managed to gain acceptance on the former French and Belgian battlefields and participate in maintaining German graves. Today there are thirty-one German cemeteries around Verdun containing the remains of men who died on both sides of the River Meuse.

In 2013 another scandalous case came to light in the Champagne region where once again building work brought up unexpected bones. Investigations at Boult-sur-Suippes led to the discovery of 527 German soldiers who had been buried with their personal effects in a wartime cemetery and which a private contractor had been paid to clear in the 1920s. Another disgrace, but one which, one hundred years after the war, is of considerable interest to archeologists. Only a few men can be identified but all, at last, will receive honoured burial.

German cemeteries such as this were cleared and the bodies exhumed for reburial. *Tom Gudmestad*

Shell damage in Verdun. *Tom Gudmestad*

The first coffins are transported into the unfinished Ossuary. *Author's collection*

German troops receiving decorations in the field. *Author's collection*

Shelling has destroyed this French 155mm gun. *Tom Gudmestad*

Advice to Tourers

Getting to Verdun: Verdun is easily reached by car from Calais via the A26 and A4. For train travellers there is the fifty-nine minute high speed TGV service from the *Gare de l'Est*, Paris, to the new Meuse TGV station, which is twenty two kilometres south of Verdun and connected to the city centre by shuttle bus.

Accommodation: The city and surrounding area offer accommodation ranging from three star hotels to self-catering cottages, bed and breakfast and camp sites. As parking in the centre of Verdun is fairly expensive, an out-of-town hotel may be a more attractive option. For a full list of accommodation, contact the tourist office or check this site: http://www.verdun-tourisme.com

Getting to the start of the tours: The tours begin at varying distances from the city at places not served by public transport. Car hire is available in Verdun but, for greater choice and the possibility of English-speaking assistance, it may be better to hire elsewhere. Ask the *Office de Tourisme* in Verdun for information about bike hire. See the **Useful Addresses** section at the back of this book for contact details.

When to travel: Summer is likely to bring the best weather but the thick forest makes it difficult to get a feel for the terrain and the mosquitoes are a nuisance. Autumn and early spring are better, particularly the latter, as by then the organized hunting season is over. Fleury Memorial Museum, the Ossuary, Fort Douaumont and Fort Vaux are closed from the third week of December to early February.

Hunting/Logging: Roughly speaking, hunting takes place on any day of the week between September and the end of February. Hunts can temporarily block access to large areas, including the main historical sites, so be prepared to choose another route if need be. Keep away from foresters using heavy logging machinery.

Firing range restrictions: Use of the firing range to the north of Fort Douaumont restricts access to the sector covered by Tours Nos 1 and 2. Current restrictions are as follows:

1 November – 14 December and 1 – 31 January:
From 1 – 7 of the month: Firing from Monday to Friday inclusive
From 8 – 21 of the month: Firing from Monday to Wednesday
inclusive

1 February – 13 July and 6 August – 31 October
From 1 – 15 of the month: Firing from Monday to Friday inclusive
From 16 – 21 of the month: Firing from Monday – Tuesday inclusive

Winter weather: Take particular care in snow and icy weather as minor roads are unlikely to be cleared, salted or gritted. This also applies to the roads across the battlefield.

Clothing/footwear: Verdun can be very wet and the forest tracks are likely to be muddy all year, so bring a rainproof jacket and wear stout, waterproof and non-slip footwear. Make sure you have appropriate medical insurance. In summer, bring plenty of mosquito repellent, including mosquito spray for your room. Cover up with long trousers and sleeves to protect against mosquitoes and ticks.

Phone signals: Make sure your phone is fully charged before you set out but be aware that the signal may be poor or even non-existant.

Refreshments/Toilets: These are very limited unless you are close to the main sites on the Right Bank. The cafés and toilets closest to Tour No 1 are in Vacherauville, which is not on the tour route. There is a café in Azannes-et-Soumazannes at the start of Tour No 2. For Tours Nos 3 and 4, refreshments and toilets are available during opening hours at Fleury Memorial Museum, the Ossuary, and the *Abri des Pèlerins* café/restaurant.

Access for visitors with limited mobility: The main memorials on the Right Bank may be reached by car but the forest tracks are inaccessible. Apart from Fleury Memorial Museum, which has a level entrance and an internal elevator, the battlefield sites are not well equipped to deal with visitors with limited mobility. The Ossuary has ramps for the main entrance but visiting the lower floor involves steps either inside or outside. Most of the interior of Fort Vaux can be visited in a wheelchair but touring the superstructure would be impossible. At the time of writing the new elevator at Fort Douaumont, which is intended to avoid the steep ramp from the car park to the entrance, is not operating and, while the ground floor of the fort is mostly level, there is no way of getting to the lower floor without negotiating steep stairs. There is also no easy way of accessing the superstructure of the fort and the paths there are not level. The *Abri des Pèlerins* café/restaurant has a ramp to the entrance.

French War Diaries *(Journaux de Marche)*:
These are held at the *Service Historique de la Défense*, Château de Vincennes, Avenue de Paris, F-94306 VINCENNES Cedex
For information see: http://www.servicehistorique.sga.defense.gouv.fr
They may be consulted online at:
http://www.memoiredeshommes.sga. defense.gouv.fr/jmo/cdc.html
These are a wonderful source of information but many are handwritten.

French Regimental Histories: *(Historiques régimentaires)*
These are to be found in *Gallica*, the digital document collection at the *Bibliothèque Nationale de France* at this link:
http://gallica.bnf.fr/ accueil.
While some French regimental histories contain detailed information, many are merely summaries.

List of *Morts pour la France*:
This is available on the website named *Mémoire des Hommes* of the French *Ministère de la Défense* through this link:
http://www.memoiredeshommes.sga.defense.gouv.fr/fr/arkotheque/client /mdh/base_morts_pour_la_france_premiere_guerre
It is not a complete list.

French war graves:
A searchable database of burial sites is available on *Mémoire des Hommes* under *Sépultures de Guerre* here:
http://www.memoiredeshommes.sga.defense.gouv.fr/fr/arkotheque/client /mdh/sepultures_guerre/
It is not complete and does not include the graves of men whose remains were returned to their families.

German regimental histories:
These are available on CD-Rom via this link:
http://www.military-books.de.vu/

A note on time: During the Battle of Verdun German time was normally one hour ahead of French time. Any specific time mentioned in this book is French time.

Separate sections at the end of this book contain information on guidebooks, other places of interest and useful addresses.

Useful Addresses

General information

Office de Tourisme: Place de la Nation, 55106 Verdun.
Tel. + 33 3 29 86 14 18
Website: www.tourisme-verdun.com
Email: contact@tourisme-verdun.com

Battlefield sites
Fort Douaumont and Fort Vaux
Current opening times and tariffs are to be found on:
www.tourisme-verdun.com
or on http://verdun-meuse.fr/index.php?qs=fr/lieux-et-visites/les-forts-de-douaumont-et-de-vaux

Please note that opening times may change without warning. Outside visits are possible at any time, including when the forts are closed.

Mémorial de Verdun (Fleury Memorial museum)
1, Ave. Du Corps Européen, 55100 Fleury-devant-Douaumon
Tel. + 33 3 29 84 35 34
http://www.memorialdeverdun.fr/

The Ossuary
55100 Douaumont, France.
Tel. + 33 3 29 84 54 81, fax + 33 3 29 86 56 54,
Mobile + 33 (0) 6 24 73 03 90
http://www.verdun-douaumont.com
Opening times are very variable, so please consult the website before visiting.

Verdun City Sites

Monument de la Victoire et au Poilu de Verdun
Rue Mazel, Verdun.
The imposing *Monument to Victory and to the Soldier of Verdun* takes the form of a cloaked and helmeted warrior who is facing east and thrusting his sword into the ground against the invader. The crypt under the monument is open from 1 April – 30 September. Entrance is free.

Citadelle Souterraine (Underground Citadel)
Avenue du 5ème R.A.P., Verdun, France.
Seven kilometres of underground galleries, forming a major logistical base throughout the Battle of Verdun. The visit also includes the room in which the French Unknown Soldier was chosen.
Tel. + 33 3 29 84 84 42
For opening times and tariffs, please consult the website:
http://www.citadelle-souterraine-verdun.fr/
Note: All visits must be reserved in advance.

Other Sites in the Area

Tranchée de Chattancourt: an interesting reconstructed **trench system** at the foot of the Mort-Homme
8 Rue de Baley, 55100 CHATTANCOURT. Tel: 06 64 77 04 67
www.tranchee-verdun.com
email: contact@tranchee-verdun.com

Camp Marguerre: A German encampment and experimental concrete production station in the Bois de Spincourt, near Muzeray.
N49°17.422' E005°34.088'

Site of 380mm 'Long Max' naval gun: Not far from Camp Marguerre in the Bois de Warphemont, near Duzey. N49°21.588' E005°36.339'

Ouvrage de la Falouse
The last permanent fieldwork to be built at Verdun, beautifully restored.
Lieu-dit Le Plat d'Houillon, 55100 Dugny-sur –Meuse, France.
N49°07.313' E005°24.037'
Tel: 06.83.27.13.34.
http://www.ouvragedelafalouse.fr/
Email: lafalouse@orange.fr
1 April – 30 September: 9 – 12 and 1.30 – 5, 1 October – 11 November 9 – 12
Other times by appointment.

Moro Lager/Camp Moreau, Vienne le Chateau
A well restored German camp. To arrange visits, contact: Maison du Pays d'Argonne, Rue St. Jacques, 51800 Vienne le Château, France, tel. + 33 3 26 60 49 40.
Email: mpa@argonne.fr
www.valleemoreau.com

Butte de Vauquois
A wonderfully preserved site, the scene of intense mine warfare, not to be missed. The craters may be visited at any time but to visit the museum and the underground installations contact:

Les Amis de Vauquois et de sa Région:
1 rue d'Orléans, 55270 Vauquois, France, http://www.butte-vauquois.fr/

Private WWI Museums

Romagne sous Montfaucon:
http://www.romagne14-18.com/index.php/en/
Extraordinary and thought provoking, also has a sandwich bar. See the website for opening times. Guided visits by appointment.

Nantillois:
http://www.14-18nantillois.com/
A great collection with a different focus from the Romagne museum. Also offers accommodation. See the website for opening times. Guided tours by appointment.

American sites

Meuse-Argonne Memorial
Montfaucon d'Argonne.
Tel: +33 (0)3 29 85 14 18
See the website for opening times:
http://www.abmc.gov/cemeteries-memorials/europe/montfaucon-american-monument

Meuse-Argonne American Cemetery and information centre
Rue de Général Pershing, 55110, Romagne-sous-Montfaucon
Tel: +33 (0)3 29 85 14 18
http://www.abmc.gov/cemeteries-memorials/europe/meuse-argonne-american-cemetery

Further Reading

These works are suggested in addition to those listed in the Select Bibliography.

On the Battle of Verdun
In English
The Price of Glory, Alistair Horne (London, Macmillan & Co. Ltd., 1962)
German Strategy and the Path to Verdun, Robert T. Foley (Cambridge University Press, 2005)
Verdun, Marshal Pétain (London, Elkin Mathews & Marrot, Ltd. 1930)
Education before Verdun, Arnold Zweig (New York, Viking, 1936)
History of the American Field Service in France 'Friends of France' 1914 – 1917, told by its Members, (Boston & New York, Houghton Mifflin Company, The Riverside Press Cambridge, 1920)
War Books, Jean Norton Cru (San Diego University Press, 1976)
Fort Douaumont – Verdun, Christina Holstein (Battleground Europe series; Barnsley, Pen & Sword Books, 2002)
Fort Vaux, Christina Holstein (Battleground Europe series; Barnsley, Pen & Sword Books, 2011)
Walking Verdun: A Guide to the Battlefield, Christina Holstein (Battleground Europe series; Barnsley, Pen & Sword Books, 2009)
The Left Bank, Christina Holstein (Battleground Europe series; Barnsley, Pen & Sword Books, 2016)

In French
Témoins, Jean Norton Cru (Presses Universitaires de Nancy, 25, rue Baron Louis, 54000 Nancy, 1993)
Verdun 1916, Jacques Péricard (Nouvelle Librairie de France, 1947)
Verdun 1916. Le point de vue français, Allain Bernède (Editions Cénomane, Le Mans, 2002)

In German
Verdun 1916: Urschlacht des Jahrhunderts, Olaf Jessen (Munich, Verlag C H Beck oHG, 2014)
Verdun: Die Schlacht und der Mythos, German Werth (Augsburg, Weltbild Verlag, 1990)
Verdun – Das Grosse Gericht, P C Ettighoffer (Gütersloh, Bertelsmann, 1936)

General background

Paths of Glory: the French Army 1914-1918, Anthony Clayton (London, Cassel Military, 2003)

My War Experiences, Crown Prince William of Germany (London, Hurst & Blackett, 1922)

American fighters in the Foreign Legion 1914 – 1918, Paul Ayres Rockwell (Boston and New York, Houghton Mifflin Company, 1930)

For interesting photographs of Verdun from French archives, see *The French Army at Verdun,* Ian Sumner (Barnsley, Pen & Sword Military, 2016)

For information on the Verdun fortress system with contemporary and new photographs, see http://www.fortiffsere.fr/

Select Bibliography

French Sources:
Les Armées Françaises dans la Grande Guerre, Service Historique,
Ministère de la Guerre, Tome IV : Verdun et la Somme, Vols.
1, 2 and 3 (Paris, Imprimerie Nationale, 1926)

War Diaries [Journaux de Marche et d'Opérations] Service
Historique de la Défense references given in brackets:

Place de Verdun
*Journal du général gouverneur (Général Coutenceau): JMO 25 juillet
1914 – 18 juillet 1915* (26N 67/1)
Fort de la Laufée: *JMO 12 mai – 31 décembre 1916* (26N 72/11)

Divisions
6ᵉ division d'infanterie: JMO 22 janvier – 25 octobre 1916
(26N 274/6)
*9ᵉ division d'infanterie, Groupe de brancardiers: JMO 2 août 1914 –
31 décembre 1916* (26N 285/15)
26ᵉ division d'infanterie: JMO 6 juin 1918 – 20 août 1919
(26N 313/6)
51ᵉ division d'infanterie: JMO 18 septembre 1914 –20 juillet 1916
(26N 366/2)
72ᵉ division d'infanterie: JMO 27 août 1915 – 12 août 1916
(26N 397/2)
74ᵉ division d'infanterie: JMO 11 novembre 1915 – 17 novembre 1916
(26N 402/3)
124ᵉ division d'infanterie : JMO 15 juin 1915 – 31 décembre 1916
(26N 425/1)

Brigades
103ᵉ brigade d'infanterie: JMO 6 juin – 22 juin 1916 (26N 524/10)
144ᵉ brigade d'infanterie: JMO 12 décembre 1915 – 31 décembre 1916
(26N 534/3)
255ᵉ brigade d'infanterie: JMO 2 avril – 31 décembre 1916
(26N 547/12)

Regiments
Colonial Infantry
41ᵉ régiment d'infanterie coloniale: JMO 27 février – 31 décembre 1916 (26N 866/19)

Infantry
5ᵉ régiment d'infanterie: JMO 1er mai 1915 – 31 décembre 1916 (26N 577/7)
11ᵉ régiment d'infanterie: JMO 22 octobre 1915 – 24 octobre 1916 (26N 585/3)
24ᵉ régiment d'infanterie: JMO 26 décembre 1915 – 31 décembre 1916 (26N 599/5)
28ᵉ régiment d'infanterie: JMO 1er mars – 31 juillet 1916 (26N 603/5)
44ᵉ régiment d'infanterie: JMO 31 juillet 1914 – 13 avril 1916 (26N 632/1) *JMO 13 avril 1916 – 20 mai 1917* (26N 632/2)
54ᵉ régiment d'infanterie: JMO 28 juin 1915 – 31 décembre 1916 (26N 644/12)
67ᵉ régiment d'infanterie: JMO 25 décembre 1914 – 31 décembre 1916 (26N 657bis/18)
75ᵉ régiment d'infanterie: JMO 10 février – 13 juillet 1916 (26N 661/5)
102ᵉ régiment d'infanterie: JMO 25 septembre 1915 – 31 décembre 1916 (26N 674/7)
106ᵉ régiment d'infanterie: JMO 1 janvier – 31 décembre 1916 (26N 677/6)
119ᵉ régiment d'infanterie: JMO 12 octobre 1914 – 10 juin 1917 (26N 683/2)
132ᵉ régiment d'infanterie: JMO 15 octobre 1915 – 7 octobre 1916 (26N 688/3)
142ᵉ régiment d'infanterie: JMO 20 janvier 1916 – 1 novembre 1917 (26N 693/15)
147ᵉ régiment d'infanterie: JMO 15 janvier – 31 décembre 1916 (26N 695/12)
154ᵉ régiment d'infanterie: JMO 1 juin 1915 – 5 février 1920 (26N 698/2)
155ᵉ régiment d'infanterie: JMO 31 mai 1916 – 20 octobre 1917 (26N 699/4)
164ᵉ régiment d'infanterie: JMO 3 juillet 1914 – 17 décembre 1914 (26N 703/1)
JMO 18 décembre 1914 – 7 mai 1915 (26N 703/2), *JMO 9 mai 1915 – 31décembre 1916* (26N 703/3)

177

167ᵉ régiment d'infanterie: JMO 2 mai 1915 – 28 janvier 1917
(26N 706/2)
168ᵉ régiment d'infanterie: JMO 28 février – 19 juillet 1916
(26N 706/7)
171ᵉ régiment d'infanterie: JMO 30 mars – 31 août 1916 (26N 708/5)
208ᵉ régiment d'infanterie: JMO 8 décembre 1915 – 31 décembre 1916
(26N 714/12)
243ᵉ régiment d'infanterie: JMO 3 janvier – 31 mai 1916 (26N 726/7)
299ᵉ régiment d'infanterie: JMO 1 janvier – 31 décembre 1916
(26N 744/2)
310ᵉ régiment d'infanterie: JMO 1 janvier – 1 juin 1916 (26N 746/17)
327ᵉ régiment d'infanterie: JMO 17 octobre 1915 – 18 juillet 1916
(26N 751/3)
333ᵉ régiment d'infanterie: JMO 2 novembre 1915 – 31 décembre 1916
(26N 754/3)
347ᵉ régiment d'infanterie: JMO 11 mars – 22 juin 1916 (26N 758/3)

Battalions
Chasseurs à pied
50ᵉ bataillon de chasseurs à pied: JMO 3 septembre – 31 décembre
1916 (26N 828/16)
56ᵉ bataillon de chasseurs à pied: JMO 4 juillet 1914 – 6 juillet 1916
(26N 830/1)
59ᵉ bataillon de chasseurs à pied: JMO 5 avril 1915 – 20 mars 1916
(26N 832/2)
71ᵉ bataillon de chasseurs à pied: JMO 31 juillet 1914 –14 juin 1918
(26N 834/16)
Tirailleurs Sénégalais
71ᵉ bataillon : JMO 28 avril 1916 –15 mars 1919 (26N 872/2)

Artillery
26ᵉ régiment d'artillerie de campagne, 2ᵉ batterie: JMO 2 août 1914 –
6 avril 1918 (26N 950/8)
60ᵉ régiment d'artillerie de campagne, 3ᵉ et 4ᵉ groupes: JMO 14 juillet
1915–31 décembre 1916 (26N 1011/13bis)
121ᵉ régiment d'artillerie lourde, 1ᵉ groupe: JMO 1 novembre 1915 –
18 mai 1916 (26N 1143/1)

Génie
6ᵉ régiment du génie, 11ᵉ bataillon, 4ᵉ compagnie: JMO 22 octobre –
31 décembre 1916 (26N 1291/12)

Regimental Histories [Historiques régimentaires]

Historique du 24ᵉ régiment d'infanterie (Charles-Lavauzelle, 1920)
http://argonnaute.u-paris10.fr/ark:/naan/925f2adbea

Historique du 28ᵉ régiment d'infanterie: Campagne 1914 – 1919
(Maurice Aune et Cie Imprimeurs, 32 rue de Bellefonds, 1920)
http://argonnaute.u-paris10.fr/ark:/naan/146f873303

Les régiments d'infanterie de Compiegne pendant la Grande Guerre –
54ᵉ, 254ᵉ, 13ᵉ Tirailleurs (Amicale des Anciens Combattants des 54ᵉ,
254ᵉ, 13ᵉ Tᵃˡ, Hôtel de Ville, Compiegne)
http://gallica.bnf.fr/ark:/12148/bpt6k6465097p

Historique du 75ᵉ régiment d'infanterie : Campagne 1914 – 1918
(Imprimerie Berger-Levrault, Nancy-Paris-Strasbourg)
http://argonnaute.u-paris10.fr/ark:/naan/3e2196b10b

Historique du 106ᵉ régiment d'infanterie pendant la guerre 1914 –
1919 (Imprimerie–Typographique A Robat, 3 rue d'Orfeuil, Chalons-
sur-Marne, 1920)
http://gallica.bnf.fr/ark:/12148/bpt6k6237019s

Historique du 147ᵉ régiment d'infanterie pendant la guerre 1914 –
1918: 2ᵉ corps d'armée, 4ᵉ division d'infanterie, 7ᵉ brigade
d'infanterie (Nancy-Paris-Strasbourg, Berger-Levrault)
http://gallica.bnf.fr/ark:/12148/bpt6k6331492p

Historique du 171ᵉ régiment d'infanterie : Campagne 1914 –1919
(Belfort-Mulhouse, Société Anonyme des Etablissements
d'Imprimerie Herbelin, Mulhouse, 1920)
http://gallica.bnf.fr/ark:/12148/bpt6k6235195w

General Background

Trois jours de Bataille. Episode des combats sous Verdun, 1 au 3 juin
1916, par M. le Commandant Quenedey. (Précis de l'Académie des
Sciences, Belles-Lettres et Arts de Rouen, 1918)

Rapport du Contre-amiral Jehenne commandant les Formations de
Marins détachés aux Armées.
http://ecole.nav.traditions.free.fr/pdf/canonniers2.pdf

Le combat du bois des Caures (21 et 22 février 1916), General Henry-
Jean Fournier, Jérôme Driant (l'Association des Amis du Musée
Driant, Hôtel de ville, 02190 Neufchâtel sur Aisne, 2016)

Le Ballet des Morts. Etat, Armée, Famille: s'occuper des corps de la
Grande Guerre, Béatrix Pau (La Librairie Vuibert, 5, allée de la 2ᵉ
D.B., 75015 Paris, 2016)

Les Forêts de la Grande Guerre. Histoire, mémoire, patrimoine, Jean-
Paul Amat (Presses de l'université Paris-Sorbonne, 2015)

German sources:
On the Battle of Verdun
Der Weltkrieg 1914-1918, Vol. 10: Die Operationen des Jahres 1916 (Berlin, E S Mittler & Sohn, 1936); Vol.11: Die Kriegführung im Herbst 1916 und im Winter 1916/17 (Berlin, E S Mittler & Sohn, 1938)
Schlachten des Weltkrieges, Vol.13: *Die Tragödie von Verdun 1916,* Part I: *Die deutsche Offensivschlacht,* Ludwig Gold
—— Vol.15: *Die Tragödie von Verdun 1916,* Parts III and IV: *Die Zermürbungsschlacht,* Part IV: *Thiaumont–Fleury,* Ludwig Gold (Oldenburg/Berlin, Verlag Gerhard Stalling, 1926 and1929

Regimental histories
Das Leibgarde-Infanterie-Regiment (1. Großherzoglich hessisches) Nr. 115 im Weltkrieg 1914-1918, Alex-Victor von Frankenberg und Ludwigsdorff (Stuttgart, Chr. Belsersche Verlagsbuchhandlung, 1921)
Leib-Grenadier-Regiment König Friedrich Wilhelm III (1. Brandenburgisches) Nr. 8 im Weltkriege, Hans Schöning (Oldenburg i. O, Verlag Gerhard Stalling, 1920)
Infanterie-Regiment Kaiser Wilhelm (2. Großherzoglich hessisches) Nr. 116, Prof. Albert Hiβ (Oldenburg i. O./Berlin, Verlag Gerhard Stalling, 1924)
Die Geschichte des Infanterie-Leibregiments Großherzogin (3. Großherzoglich hessisches) Nr. 117, Hauptmann Offenbächer (Kurt) (Druck der Mainzer Verlagsanstalt und Druckerei A.-G., Oldenburg i. O., Verlag Gerhard Stalling, 1931)
3. Rheinisches Pionier-Bataillon Nr. 30, Karl Witte (Oldenburg i. O./Berlin, Verlag Gerhard Stalling, 1928)
Die vom Douaumont: Das Ruppiner Regiment 24 im Weltkrieg, Cordt v. Brandis (Berlin SW 48, Verlag Tradition Wilhelm Rolf, 1930)
Geschichte des Infanterie-Regiments Generalfeldmarschall Prinz Friedrich Karl von Preußen (8. Brandenburg.) Nr. 64, (Berlin SW 48, Verlag Tradition Wilhelm Rolf, 1929)
Sanitätsbericht über das Deutsche Heer (Deutsches Feld-und Besatzungsheer) im Weltkriege 1914/1918, II Band, (Berlin SW 68, Verlag von E S Mittler & Sohn, 1938)
Das Kgl. Sächs. 6. Infanterie-Regiment Nr. 105 König Wilhelm II. Von Württemberg, Oberlt. d. Res. A. D. Glogowsk, (Dresden, Verlag Wilhelm und Bertha v. Baensch Stiftung, 1929)
Königl. Preuß. Sturm-Bataillon Nr. 5 (Rohr), Graf Eberhard v. Schwerin (Zeulenroda (Thüringen) Druck und Verlag von Bernhard Sporn, 1939)

Grenadier-Regiment König Friedrich Wilhelm I. (2. Ostpreußishces)
Nr. 3 im Weltkriege 1914-1918, Dr. Fritz Schillmann (Oldenburg i.
O./Berlin, Druck und Verlag von Gerhard Stalling, 1924)
Geschichte des 9. Rheinischen Infanterie-Regiments Nr. 160 im
Weltkriege 1914–1918, (Zeulenroda, Verlag Sporn,1932
Geschichte der Brigade-Ersatz-Bataillone 32, 80 und 86 und des aus
diesen hervorgegangenen preuß. Infanterie-Regiments Nr. 363
während des Krieges 1914/18, Ernst Büttner (Zeulenroda
(Thüringen) Bernhard Sporn Verlag, 1937)

Index

183

Pierrepont, 163
Poncet, Léon, 148
Poudrière, 112, 124–8, 143
Poulet, Henry, 76, 98–100, 102
Poulet memorial, 102–103
Poulet, Robert, 76, 98–100, 102

Quenedey, Major, 120, 125, 130
Quenet, Julien, 1, 29–30

Rachel, André, 112, 122, 124–5
Ravin de Bazil, 112, 130–1, 137, 144
Ravin de la Caillette, 132–3, 141–2
Ravin de la Fausse Côte, 132, 136
Ravin de la Poudrière, 112, 122, 150–1
Ravin des Renards, 40, 73
Ravin des Vignes, 150
Red Zone, 48, 80, 154, 156, 158–9
Rembercourt-aux-Pots military cemetery, 134
Renouard, Etienne, 1, 18–19
Rheims, 4, 149
Riedel, Paul, 66
Roiné, René, 112, 129
Rolland, Guillaume, 16
Romagne-sous-les-Côtes, 163
Romagne-sous-Montfaucon, xix
Rudrauf, Charles, 163
Ruèche, Henri, 112, 120–1

Salamite, Jacques, 112, 120–1
Schneidercit, Otto, viii, 40, 67, 134

Sedan, 4–5, 7
Sidi Brahim, 16
Signal de la Caillette, 142–3
Sommepy-Tahure military cemetery, 134
Sommières, Paul, 112, 136–7, 141, 143
Souvenir Français, 121
St André Farm, 74
St Jean Baptiste, 119, 152
St Michel Ridge, 112, 120
Stollbrock, Bernhard, 40, 67, 134
Sturm, Leonhard, 131
Stützpunkt Hölle *see* Petit Dépôt

Tavannes tunnel, 95, 98, 110
Thébia, Augustin, 140
Thiaumont Farm, 144–5
Thiaumont fieldwork, 140
Thiaumont Redoubt, 143
Tunisia, 5

Vacherauville, 1, 37, 168
Vaux, 68, 154–6
Versailles Treaty, 164
Ville-devant-Chaumont, 1, 37, 67

Wavrille Hill, 1, 22–6, 28, 31–3, 35–6, 63, 71
Weilenmann, Paul, 40, 68–9
Winckelmann, Hans, xix
Winckelmann, Karl, xix
Wirtz, Wilhelm, 40, 68
Woëvre Plain, 44, 89, 131
Wolff, Johannes, 64